THIS BOOK is to
commemorate the issuance of the
Otoe-Missouria Medal
May 1, 1976
and is limited to 15,000 copies
No. 5861

Kenneth E. Beach

Indian Tribal Series Historical Collect

THE OTOE-MISSOURIA LEADER *Chon-ca-pe,* or "Big Kansas," as depicted in a lithograph *The Indian Tribes of North America* by Thomas L. McKenney and James Hall. This ch reportedly possessed a "temper like gunpowder" but was a shrewd warchief and effecti leader of his kinsmen.

THE OTOE-MISSOURIA PEOPLE

by R. David Edmunds

Scientific Editor: Henry F. Dobyns
General Editor: John I. Griffin

PUBLISHED BY INDIAN TRIBAL SERIES / PHOENIX

Library of Congress Catalog Number 76-19831

PRINTED IN THE UNITED STATES OF AMERICA — Imperial Lithographers

FOREWORD

It is with appreciation and pride that the history of the Otoe-Missouria people is being presented in a concise and factual manner. The Otoe-Missouria Tribal Council, composed of Hilda Harris, Julia Tah, Browning Pipestem, Kenneth Harragarra, Richard Kihega, and Logan DeRoin expressed their interest and desire to enhance and broaden the scope of our cultural background by providing our future generations with documentary materials so that our rich heritage and history would not be lost.

The author, Dr. R. David Edmunds, TCU History Department, Texas and Mr. John Griffin, Phoenix, Arizona, are the force which we owe great debt to gratitude for they have spent many hours of research and have compiled the historical data of our people in their movements and dealings with the government, settlers, and the westward movement of civilization.

We are aware of limitations of an historical account that many people had a part in various activities of a specific action, but the Otoe-Missouria people have always entered into and accomplished activities together in a team effort and respectable formalities.

It is with this thought that whatever the future holds for our people that every endeavor undertaken, that our people enter it together and with the help of Wakanda, and cannot fail.

We pray that our people and those who helped us in meeting our objectives be blessed with long life and good health.

On behalf of the Otoe-Missouria people, our office extends a special thank you to Dr. Dave Edmunds and Mr. Griffin for the exceptional contribution they have made to our people.

Kenneth E. Black, Chairman
Otoe-Missouria Tribe

ENNETH E. BLACK, Chairman, Otoe-Missouria Tribe

ABOUT THE TRIBAL CHAIRMAN

Born into the Elk Clan at Red Rock, Oklahoma, on June 13, 1923, Kenneth E. Black, whose tribal name is *Wangieewajo*, is the son of Albert and Ada Shadlow Black, prominent members of the Otoe-Missouria community. Growing up within the old tribal reservation, Black attended the public elementary school at Red Rock and later enrolled at Haskell Indian Institute. In 1942, upon his graduation from Haskell, Black enlisted in the Army Air Corps, spending the next two years in combat in the South Pacific.

Following World War II, Black was employed by the city of Enid, Oklahoma, and later worked for the Department of Education of the Bureau of Indian Affairs where his duties included counseling Indian students. More recently, he has served as the Executive Director of the United Tribes of Western Oklahoma and Kansas, coordinating the administration of the twenty-three tribes who comprise the association. A veteran of seventeen years experience on the Otoe-Missouria Tribal Council, in 1972 Black was elected chairman of the organization. During his term as chairman, permanent tribal offices have been established at Red Rock and a series of economic and educational programs have been implemented. Dedicated to serving his people, Kenneth Black continues to provide an active leadership for the Otoe-Missouria Tribe.

In 1954, Black married the former Mary Jane Harjo, a full-blood Creek and the couple are parents of twin daughters, Doris and Delores, who attend Oklahoma State University. The Black family resides in Shawnee, Oklahoma.

Five centuries ago, while the pale skinned invaders still slept beyond the eastern sea, a large tribe of Siouan speaking people left their lodges on the northern shores of the Great Lakes and journeyed south, seeking new homes in a region free from the snows of Canada. Passing down the western shores of Lake Michigan, the emigrants came upon an immense bay teeming with fish and waterfowl. Attracted by the abundant food supply, part of the people (the Winnebagos) chose to remain in the area, but the others continued westward until they reached the banks of a large river called Mississippi or "Great River" by nearby Algonquian tribesmen. The wanderers followed the Mississippi south, but near the mouth of the Rock River, the Iowa or "Gray Snow People" separated from the other Indians, establishing villages near modern Rock Island.

The remaining tribesmen crossed the Mississippi and trekked on to the southwest, eventually reaching the Missouri near its juncture with the Grand River. Exhausted from their travels, the people pitched their lodges along the river bottom, intending to settle permanently in the region. The harmony of the new village soon was disrupted by a quarrel which divided the people into opposing factions. Impressed by the beauty of one of the village women, a young war chief asked for her hand in marriage, but the girl's family spurned his offer, rejecting his bridal payments. In defiance, the couple met secretly in the forest, consummating their relationship. When the girl's father learned of their love-making he became angry, threatening to attack the young man's family. The people then divided, part of the villagers following the young chief and his kinsmen up the Missouri Valley. Other members of the tribe accompanied the woman's father to a new town at the mouth of the Missouri River. Because the young woman left her family and joined her lover, the tribesmen who journeyed upstream were known as "Wahtohtana" or "Those Who Make Love" (the Otoes). The woman's relatives received the name "Neotacha" or "People of the River's Mouth" (the Missourias).

For the Otoes, the trip up the Missouri River was a pleasant experience. They followed the broad stream past the mouth of the Kansas and then turned north, camping beside the river as it skirted the western flanks of the Blacksnake Hills. Continuing upstream, they passed along the western bank of the

Missouri until they were stopped by a tributary which entered the Missouri from the plains. The region abounded with game and the fertile soil of the river valley promised good crops of corn, beans, and pumpkins. Satisfied with the location, the Otoes named the western river "Nemaha" or "Water of Cultivation" and erected permanent villages near its confluence with the Missouri.

The lower Nemaha Valley proved to be an excellent homeland. Assisted by Otoe warriors, the village women cleared small fields along the river bottoms and planted the sacred seed corn which had been saved from the past year's harvest. They also sowed crops of beans, melons, squash, and pumpkins, carefully cultivating the soil with large hoes made from wood and buffalo scapulae. In mid-summer, the corn was harvested and the Green Corn Festival took place. After the celebration, the remaining corn was dried and stored for the winter, a portion being saved for the next year's planting. Beans and squash also were dried, but pumpkins first were roasted and pulled apart, then cut into strips and left in the sun until the meat hardened, preserving the strips almost indefinitely. The Otoes supplemented their crops with wild plant foods gathered from the nearby plains and forests.

While the women cared for the gardens, Otoe hunters stalked deer and elk in the forests that filled the river valleys. They also hunted smaller game, taking raccoons and rabbits from the thickets and killing ducks and geese while the birds rested on

FOUR OTOE-MISSOURIA HORSEMEN posing on the Plains, showing the approximate appea

Courtesy of the Western History Collections, University of Oklahoma Library

r buffalo ponies, along with later horse-gear including manufactured bridles and saddles.

backwaters along the river. Yet the deer and small game were only part of the Otoes' meat supply, for twice each year, in the spring and fall, they ventured onto the plains to hunt buffalo. The buffalo hunts were well organized expeditions in which most of the tribe participated. The spring hunt was controlled by the Buffalo Clan, a group of inter-related families who led the tribe during the spring and summer. The autumn hunt was directed by the Bear Clan, another important group of Otoe families.

In the early period, the Otoes attempted to stampede the buffalo herds over cliffs, but after they acquired horses Otoe warriors pursued the herds, killing fat cows and calves from horseback. When the hunt was finished, the women butchered the fallen animals, drying and packing the meat which was carried back to the villages.

The Otoe villages were small groupings of lodges strung along the Nemaha and Missouri Rivers. Although the Otoes lived in skin tents while on the plains, their permanent homes were comfortable earth lodges, almost forty feet in diameter. After excavating the area of the house to a depth of about three feet, the Otoes erected four large posts, approximately twenty feet high in the center of the circle. A series of forked poles were then set around the perimeter of the pit, and rafters were placed between the poles and the center posts. The rafters then were interlaced with sticks and the entire structure covered with earth and sod, resulting in a watertight dwelling, warm in winter and cool in summer.

A hole at the top of the lodge allowed smoke to escape, and a doorway and ramp provided access in or out of the lodge. The houses were well constructed and supported the weight of Otoe children who often played on the rooftops.

Most of the villages held related families for blood ties have always been important to the Otoe-Missouria people. The Otoes were divided into a series of clans who each traced their lineage back to a sacred bird or animal. Each clan held certain rights and responsibilities within the tribe and each provided leaders for religious or ceremonial occasions. The Buffalo People led the tribe on the spring hunt; the Bear People controlled the buffalo hunt in the fall. The Beaver People supplied the sacred pipe; the Elk People provided the fire with which the pipe was lighted. Within the clan structure, the family units remained important and individual Otoes held strong attachments toward their relatives. Much of the social and economic activity of the tribe was carried on by kinship groups so all the Otoe people shared in the triumphs and failures of the family to which they belonged.

Inasmuch as family ties were fundamentally important, many members of a family helped to care for the Otoe children. Grandparents, aunts, and uncles all shared responsibility with a child's parents for the proper upbringing of an Otoe boy or girl. Especially important was the relationship between an Otoe boy and his mother's brother, because the uncle gave the boy a nickname and was expected to offer him advice upon important matters. The uncle also was obligated to watch over the boy when he went on the warpath, and if necessary, to defend his nephew at the risk of his own life.

Children were much desired among the Otoes and although they were taught to respect their elders and to obey the customs of the tribe, the youngsters rarely were subjected to strict discipline. Believing that their children could learn best by example, the Otoes encouraged the youngsters to model themselves after responsible adults. Boys were given miniature bows and arrows and instructed to hunt rabbits and other small game. Girls helped their mothers and older sisters with household chores, preparing for the duties they would assume after marriage.

As they entered adolescence, the Otoe youths passed through ceremonies which left their childhood behind. Otoe boys ventured into the forest to fast and to seek a vision which would provide them with guidance for their roles as hunters and warriors. Appealing to *Wakonta* and other supernatural forces in the universe, the Otoe youths asked for their blessings and promised to faithfully serve both their family and the tribe. When Otoe girls became sexually mature their families held feasts in their honor and the girl's mother and grandmother prepared the young woman for her formal entrance into the responsibilities of adult life. At the onset of her first menstrual period, the girl also fasted and secluded herself in a special hut which was erected behind her family's lodge. Her grandmother assured the young woman that she now could marry and have children, but warned her to avoid family members during her monthly periods. The Otoes believed that too close an association with a menstruating woman could cause hunters to find no game and that her condition brought bad luck to those who were ill or injured.

Otoe marriages usually were arranged by older family members and neither bride nor groom played a major part in choosing their future mate. Marriage between men and women of the same clan was forbidden, but parents hoped to marry their children to members of rich or influential families outside their clan. The proposal was made by the groom's father who offered horses or other goods to the family of the bride. If the offer was accepted, the wedding celebration eventually took place and the young couple lived with the bride's parents until the birth of their first child. After the baby was born, the couple established their own lodge in the village of the woman's parents. Like other prairie peoples, the Otoe and Missourias developed formal rules to govern the relationship between in-laws. To minimize friction, an Otoe man avoided his mother-in-law and spoke to his father-in-law only about matters of importance. The restraints upon an Otoe woman were less severe, but she treated both her husband's parents with more respect than familiarity.

The political leadership of the Otoe-Missouria people also reflected their strong kinship affiliations. Each of the clans was led by hereditary chiefs who joined together to form a tribal council. In the early period, the Otoes also were guided by a tribal chief who traditionally came from the Bear Clan, but who exercised only limited authority. In reality the political power of all the Otoe leaders rested upon their ability to reflect the will or consensus of clan or tribal members. Both clan and tribal chiefs had only limited powers of coercion over their followers and were forced to rely upon family members to keep order in the villages. The tribal council concerned itself primarily with domestic affairs and in the early period the clan and tribal chiefs took little part in inter-tribal warfare. Then in the nineteenth century, as the tribe found its villages threatened by both red and white enemies, the traditional chiefs took a major role in defending the Otoe homeland.

When a prominent Otoe chief or warrior died, his family and the tribe held extensive ceremonies to honor his memory. For four days after the man's death the village remained in mourning, his relatives and close friends sometimes slashing themselves with knives to signify their grief over the loss. Most of the dead man's possessions were distributed to close friends or clan members and a feast was held to commemorate his passing. The dead man was dressed in his finest clothing and painted with his clan's insignia, his body being laid out in his lodge. On the second or third day after his death, the body was interred, either wrapped in a blanket and placed in a tree, or buried in the ground, facing north, the land of the spirits. Meanwhile, the man's favorite horse was killed and its skull placed in the grave, providing the dead warrior with transportation for his journey to the spirit world.

The Otoes and Missourias believed that both the spirit world and the world of men were governed by *Wakonta*, the supreme power in the universe. *Wakonta's* presence was everywhere, inhabiting both living and inanimate objects. Also present were a host of other supernatural forces which the Otoes took pains not to anger. The Otoe people knew that certain dreams and visions gave some tribal members insight into the spirit world, enabling them to prophesy both good and evil. They also believed that certain individuals possessed strong medicine, investing them with the power to cure specific injuries or diseases. Other maladies were treated by tribal societies or "lodges." The Buffalo Doctors' Lodge knew how to set broken bones; the Buffalo Lodge assisted women in childbirth. The Snake Doctors cured snake bites; the Red Bean Medicine Lodge prepared purgatives. All of the lodges and secret societies periodically held dances and ceremonies, both propitiating the spirits and providing enjoyable social occasions for tribe members.

A congenial people, the Otoes and Missourias met often for dances and games. The Buffalo Moccasin Lodge held dances at which gifts were given to needy members of the tribe. The Peace Pipe Dance was performed to formalize peace with neighboring tribes. Both men and women also enjoyed playing several games in which the competition was sometimes fierce, but friendly. In the spring, Otoe war-

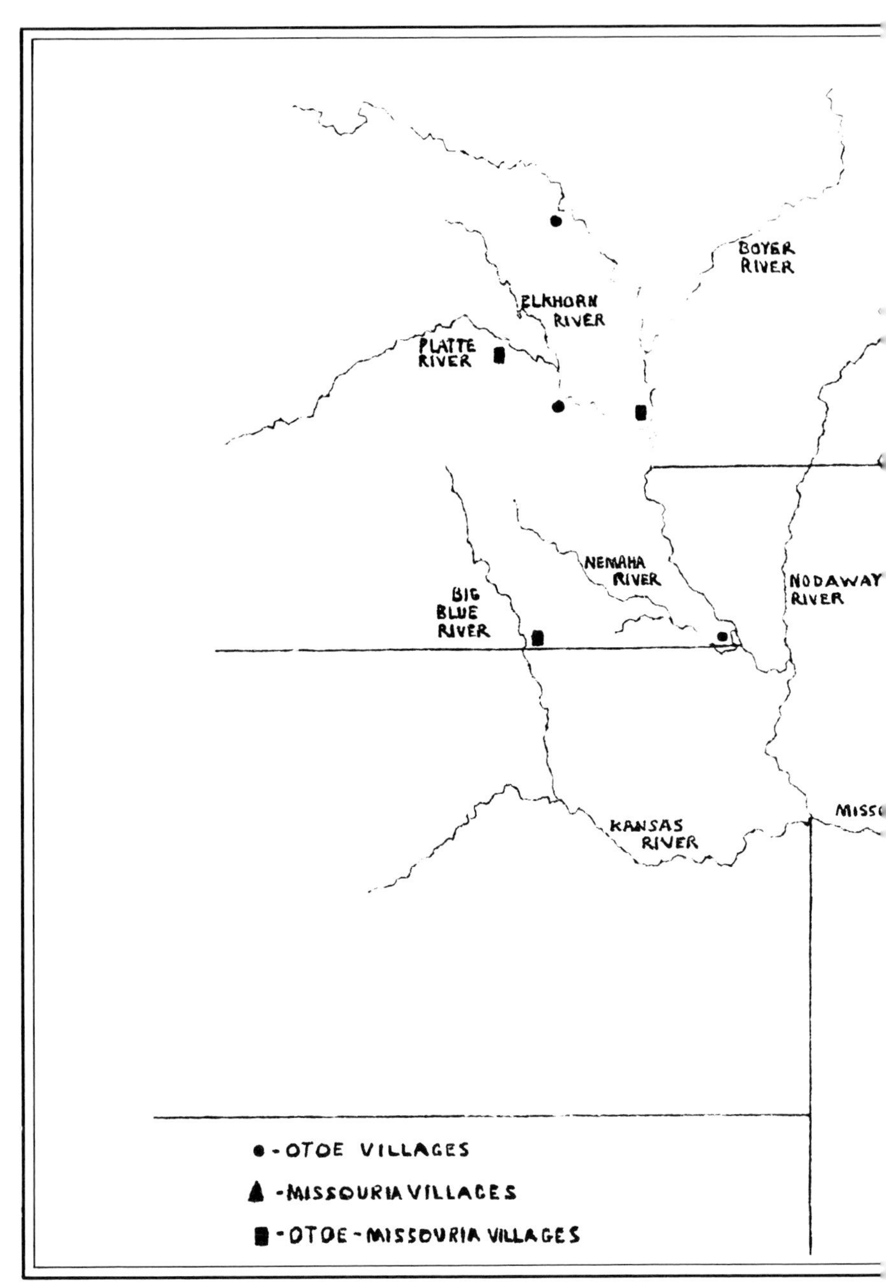
BOYER RIVER
ELKHORN RIVER
PLATTE RIVER
NEMAHA RIVER
NODAWAY RIVER
BIG BLUE RIVER
KANSAS RIVER
● - OTOE VILLAGES
▲ - MISSOURIA VILLAGES
■ - OTOE - MISSOURIA VILLAGES

MAP 1.

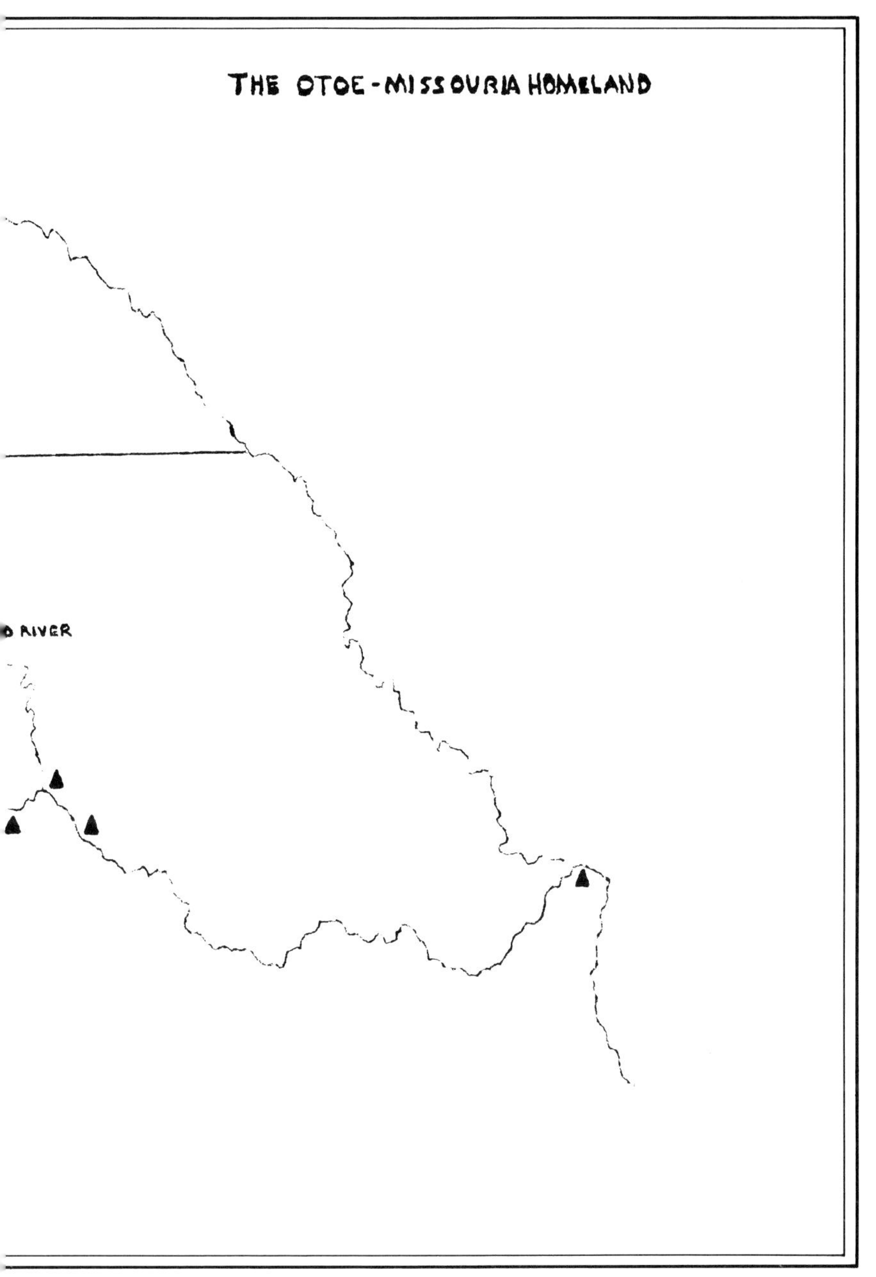

Map by Tom Boyd

riors played the sacred ball game which resembled the modern sport of lacrosse. Although women did not participate in the contest, they took part in the victory dance which followed. Men also competed in throwing spears at rolling hoops, and women played a separate ball game, utilizing short poles and a ball made of buffalo sinew. Both sexes played the hand ball game and both took pleasure in gambling with bone dice, a pastime that was widely popular among both the Otoe and Missouria tribes.

Early white travelers along the Missouri and Platte rivers generally described the Otoes and Missourias in favorable terms. Although the Otoe-Missouria people consistently were outnumbered by many of the surrounding tribes, they ably protected their hunting lands from enemy warriors. One American observer noted that most Otoe men bore scars won in numerous battles against Sioux or Osage raiders and that the Otoe-Missouria warriors were "probably the bravest of the native inhabitants of the Missouri." Other whites commented upon the tribe's superb horsemanship, adding that "the character of the Otoe tribe for furious courage, and pre-eminent skill with the rifle" had earned them the respect of their enemies.

The diaries and journals of white observers also provide valuable descriptions of the Indians' physical appearance and clothing. Of average height, Otoe-Missouria warriors were depicted as robust, muscular men with "frank and gallant bearings." During the warm months, warriors often went without clothing except for a breechcloth and moccasins. In the winter they added a loose, fringed, deerskin hunting shirt and leggings, wrapping themselves in a buffalo robe or blanket as protection against the cold. Although Otoe warriors usually shaved their heads except for a scalp-lock, some of the men wore their hair long, keeping it in place with a head-band of animal skin. Eager to enhance their appearance, the men adorned their faces and bodies with paint, usually black or vermilion. They also wore extensive jewelry, piercing their ears for short strings of beads and bedecking themselves with necklaces of bear-claws.

Otoe-Missouria women wore moccasins and loose-fitting one piece deerskin dresses that extended below their knees. Like their husbands, during the winter they wrapped themselves in buffalo robes or blankets. Very young Otoe-Missouria children were dressed in a short shirt, but after they reached four or five years of age, boys' and girls' clothing resembled that worn by their elders. As the tribe established closer ties with white traders, they began to substitute cotton or wool cloth for the more traditional deerskin clothing, decorating their brightly colored shirts and dresses with large brass or silver buckles and buttons.

THE MISSOURIAS, 1690-1800

In the prehistoric period, after the Missourias and Otoes had divided, the Missourias established a temporary village near the juncture of the Missouri and

Mississippi Rivers, but by the middle of the seventeenth century they had moved their village back upstream, re-occupying lands near the mouth of the Grand. Sometime prior to 1690, the Missouria tribesmen were visited by Kaskaskia warriors from Illinois, bringing news of a strange new people who were active among the tribes of Wisconsin. The Kaskaskias described the newcomers in wonderous terms, telling of their pale complexions and the marvelous things they were willing to trade for beaver pelts. Anxious to meet the strangers, the Missourias asked their visitors from Illinois to bring the new people to their village, promising to provide the foreigners with as many beaver pelts as they wanted.

In 1693, the Kaskaskias honored the Missourias' request, guiding a small party of Frenchmen up the river to the Missouria village. The French were impressed with the Missourias' fur and a brisk trade soon developed, the Missourias crossing over the Mississippi to carry their pelts to French posts in Illinois. Unfortunately for the Missourias, French traders also extended their commerce to the Sacs and Foxes, enemy tribes from the upper Mississippi Valley who long had been at war with the Missourias. Well armed by French merchants, Fox warriors descended into the Missouria homeland, killing isolated hunters and occasionally attacking Missouria villages. Angered by the incursions, the Missourias struck back, and in 1712, when the Foxes and French quarreled near Detroit, the Missourias sent

Courtesy of the Western History Collections, University of Oklahoma Library

)RTRAIT OF OTOE-MISSOURIA CHIEF Medicine Horse wearing bear-claw necklace, beads, rrings, with trade tomahawk and blanket. With no shirt on, Medicine Horse closely sembled the aboriginal warrior.

warriors to Michigan who assisted the French in annihilating a large war party of Foxes and Mascoutens.

After the Missourias returned from Detroit, their ties with the French increased. Etienne V. De Bourgmont, a young French officer, accompanied the Missouria warriors back to their village where he lived for several years, taking a Missouria wife and exploring the lower Missouri River Valley. Other French agents passed through their villages and in 1723 De Bourgmont constructed a French post, Fort Orleans, on the Missouri River, a few miles above the mouth of the Grand. The Missourias moved their village near to the pallisade and in 1724 they accompanied several Frenchmen who traveled west onto the plains of Kansas, extending French trade to the Comanches. In gratitude, during 1725 De Bourgmont included several Missouria warriors and at least one Missouria woman in a delegation of Indians he escorted to France, where the Missourias toured Paris and were presented at the court of Louis XV. They returned to North America in 1727.

After 1730, the Missouria-French relationship declined. In 1729, the French abandoned Fort Orleans, consolidating their strength along the Mississippi where they turned their attention toward the Chickasaws. Encouraged by the French retreat, the Sacs renewed their war against the Missourias and during 1730 a large Sac war party successfully eluded Missouria scouts and surprised the village located near the abandoned Fort Orleans. Although the Missouria warriors fought desperately, they were overwhelmed and almost 300 of their tribesmen were killed by the raiders.

Recoiling from the attack, the Missouria people met in council and concluded that they no longer could put their trust in French protection. Seeking new friends, the Missourias turned to the Osages, also enemies of the Sacs, and suggested that the two tribes join together for defense against their common foes. The Osages welcomed the Missouria proposal and invited the survivors of the Sac attack to cross over to the south side of the Missouri River, offering them a site for a new village near the Little Osage town, about twenty-five miles upstream from the mouth of the Grand.

Accepting the Osage offer, the Missourias erected a new town near the Little Osages. Yet the years following 1730 were not happy ones for the Missouria people. No longer self-sufficient, they continued to trade with the French for the necessities of life while continually depleting the supply of fur bearing animals in their homeland. Trade goods were not the only thing they received from the Europeans. Housed in their sedentary villages, the Missouria people were particularly susceptible to the white man's diseases and during the eighteenth century they fell victim to several epidemics that raged among the tribes of the Mississippi and lower Missouri Valleys. Moreover, their war with the Sacs continued, and while the number of Missouria warriors grew smaller, their enemies increased in strength. After the 1730's, the Sac and Fox tribes combined, and assisted by the Iowas, Kickapoos, and Potawatomis, they expanded their warfare against the Missourias and Osages. In the last third of the century, when the Spaniards replaced the French in Louisiana, they tried to bring peace to the warring tribes but achieved little success. Although the Missourias cooperated with the Spanish efforts, their enemies persisted in the conflict, reducing the once populous Missouria people to a remnant of their former strength.

The final blow fell in 1796. While enroute down the Missouri River in canoes, the remaining Missourias were ambushed by a large war party of Sacs and Foxes. Concealed among the willows along the river bank, the attackers poured a deadly fire in upon the Missouria warriors and then charged into the water, capsizing the canoes and drowning many of the Missouria women and children. Large numbers of Missourias were killed and the survivors turned to other tribes for protection. A few joined with the Little Osages or the Kansas, but most of the remaining Missourias sought refuge among the Otoes, fleeing to the Otoe village on the Platte River in modern Nebraska. The Otoes accepted their former kinsmen, and although the Missourias maintained their separate identity, after 1800 the two peoples acted as one tribe in military and political affairs. Old World diseases had taken such a toll of the Otoe and Missouria populations that severe battle losses forced them to unite to survive.

Courtesy Amon Carter Museum, Fort Worth, Texas

HIEF *ARKEKETAH,* or "Stand By It." This portrait illustrates the enduring influence of the rly fur trade: a trade tomahawk, blanket, shirt and jewelry. Yet it also shows the strength of lains artisanry in a buffalo-horn helmet with feathers and a beautiful bear-claw necklace. *rkeketah* signed the Washington Treaty of 1854 and led the Otoe-Missouria people to the ig Blue Reservation.

At the end of the seventeenth century, while the Missourias were meeting with French traders from Illinois, the Otoes abandoned their old villages on the Nemaha. Moving up the Missouri, the Otoe people reached the mouth of the Platte, where part of the tribe turned west, following the broad, shallow river till they came to Salt Creek, about thirty miles upstream from the Missouri. There, on a low hill overlooking the southwest bank of the river, they established a new village. Meanwhile, other Otoes separated from their kinsmen and continued north up the Missouri into western Iowa where they lived for several years near the Iowas.

From the Iowas and Missourias, the Otoes learned of the French occupation of Illinois and by 1700 small parties of Otoe warriors regularly were crossing the Mississippi, bartering beaver pelts for knives and other metal utensils. Calling the light-skinned strangers "Mahsonkka" or "Makers of Iron," the Otoes informed the Frenchmen that the Comanches and other western enemies were trading with the Spaniards in New Mexico. The Otoes also asked that French traders be sent to their village. Alarmed by the Otoe reports, the French warned the warriors to reject the Spaniards, and in 1714, after Bourgmont settled among the Missourias, several traders journeyed into the Otoe country.

The Otoes welcomed the Frenchmen into their village, establishing an informal alliance with New

France. In 1720, they demonstrated their loyalty to Bourgmont and other French officials by joining with the Pawnees to attack a Spanish expedition that had penetrated into Nebraska. Led by Pedro de Villasur, the Spanish party of over 100 men left Santa Fe during June, 1720, traveling northeastward across the plains in search of illegal French traders. In early August Villasur's expedition crossed the Platte River in Nebraska where it encountered the Pawnees, a nation also trading with the French. Although the Pawnee chiefs met with Villasur, the Pawnees sent riders to the Otoe village asking for warriors willing to join in an attack upon the Spaniards. The Otoes responded favorably and at daybreak on August 13, 1720, a combined war party of Otoes and Pawnees struck the Spanish encampment, scattering the intruders' horse herd. Despite a desperate defense by Villasur and his men, the Otoe and Pawnee warriors encircled their enemy, cutting the Spaniards down with arrows and musket fire. About sixty of Villasur's men eventually fled to the south, but the Spanish commander and four dozen of his followers were left dead upon the battlefield.

After the battle Otoe messengers carried news of the victory to the French in Illinois. Although the French congratulated the Otoes on their success, they were concerned about the growth of Spanish influence among the plains tribes, especially the Comanches. Inasmuch as the Otoes, Pawnees, and other Missouri River tribes were at war with the Comanches, the French supplied their allies with arms, but their support of the Otoes isolated the French from the Comanches, giving the Spaniards a free hand on the plains. Anxious to both limit Spanish authority and to extend French trade to the Comanches, French officials sought the assistance of the Otoes, Missourias, and other Indians in an effort to bring peace between the plains Indians and the river tribes. The Otoes and Missourias reluctantly agreed to assist the French, and in 1724 both tribes joined with other tribesmen to escort a French peace mission to the Comanche village in central Kansas. Led by Bourgmont, the French emissaries met with tribal leaders and in October, 1724, a tentative peace between the Otoes, Missourias, and the Comanches was arranged.

Yet the new peace did not strengthen Otoe ties with New France. Both the Otoe and Missouria leaders were suspicious that their former Comanche enemies might use the French trade to acquire more firearms for future attacks upon Otoe villages. Moreover, during the 1730's, French influence along the Missouri River declined as French officials in Illinois turned their attention to problems in the Ohio and Mississippi Valleys. Unfortunately for the Otoes, responsible Frenchmen such as Bourgmont were replaced by "coureurs de bois," lawless French traders more interested in quick profits than in trading honestly with the Indians.

At first the Otoes attempted to flee from the coureurs de bois, abandoning their village on the Platte and moving to the west bank of the Missouri in northwestern Nebraska. Yet their flight was useless for by the mid-eighteenth century both the Otoe and Missouria people relied upon European traders for the many necessities of life. Firearms, steel knives, and metal utensils, which once had been luxuries, were now needed by the tribesmen for hunting and other daily activities. They resented the shoddy goods and high prices of the coureurs de bois, but their requests for other traders were ignored by French officials more concerned about the British on the Ohio than the fur trade further west.

In 1763, when Louisiana passed into the hands of Spain, the Otoes and Missourias welcomed the news with much celebration. Although the Spaniards did not immediately occupy the Missouri Valley, both tribes hoped that the new regime would regulate the fur trade and provide them with inexpensive trade goods. Anxious to be closer to the Spaniards, the Otoes left their village on the Missouri and returned to the Platte. Their occupation of northeastern Nebraska had not been happy, for they had quarreled with the Poncas and Iowas, and Otoe chiefs such as La Bala or "The Bullet" hoped that the move would separate the tribe from potential enemies, reducing the chance for warfare along the Missouri Valley.

Eager to assert their control over the Missouri River tribes, in 1767 Spanish officials at St. Louis licensed Creole traders to venture among both the Otoes and Missourias. The merchants not only carried Spanish gifts for tribal leaders, they also received instructions limiting the prices to be charged for trade goods bartered to the Otoes and Missourias. Spanish officials, meanwhile, attempted to force the lawless coureurs de bois from "His Catholic Majesty's territory."

The Spanish efforts among the Otoes met with only limited success. The Otoes welcomed the opportunity to acquire Spanish trade goods at reasonable prices, but they opposed the efforts of Spanish traders to pass up the Missouri and trade with the tribes in the Dakotas. Some of the northern Indians, especially the Sioux, were at war with the Otoes and tribal leaders did not want their enemies well armed with Spanish weapons. In addition, the Otoes themselves traded with such tribes as the Poncas and Omahas, and shrewd Otoe middlemen resented the potential competition of Spanish merchants.

Other factors also restricted Spanish influence among the Otoe people. By the late 1770's British merchants from Canada had passed through the Great Lakes and penetrated as far west as the Missouri Valley. At first the Otoes opposed these new Mahsonkka who threatened their trade with the Omahas, but the British merchants carried such an ample supply of durable, inexpensive trade goods that the Otoes soon forgot their plans for a trade monopoly in their efforts to lure British traders to their village. In 1778, the Otoes welcomed two British merchants into their town on the Platte and during the next decade Otoe warriors became increasingly dependent upon British gunpowder furnished by traders from Canada. Although Spanish officials in St. Louis tried to stop the British trade, they were unsuccessful, for the Otoes preferred the less expensive British goods and Spanish authority was limited to the lower Missouri River Valley.

In 1795, the Spaniards finally made a concerted effort to dislodge the British traders and reassert Spanish influence among the Otoe people. Working through a Spanish trading firm, the Missouri Company, Governor Carondelet of Louisiana decided to establish a series of small forts along the Missouri River, including a post at the mouth of the Platte. Carondelet hoped that the fort on the Platte would both limit British influence and induce the Otoes to trade with Spanish merchants.

During the fall of 1795, James Mackay, a naturalized Spaniard employed by the Missouri Company, met with the Otoes on the Platte, promising them that the Spanish would build a fort and trading post at the river's mouth which would supply them with guns and protect them from their enemies. Although the Otoes agreed to move their village near to the new Spanish fort, they complained about recent Spanish traders who charged high prices for their merchandise. Otoe chiefs admitted that some of their young men occasionally had robbed Spanish traders, but they promised that such practices would cease. Mackay reported back to his superiors that the Otoes were not a numerous people, yet the Missouri Company should cultivate their friendship for their strategic position near the mouth of the Platte could make them "dangerous enemies of all the commerce of the Upper Missouri."

The good intentions of the Spanish never materialized. Although the Missouri Company established several forts along the Missouri River, the post at the mouth of the Platte was forgotten. Angered over the broken promise, the Otoes, now joined by the Missourias, lashed out at Spanish shipping, seizing the goods of Spanish merchants who dared to venture near their village. In 1797, the Missouri Company attempted to appease the tribesmen, sending Francisco Derouin, a company trader, to the Otoe-Missouria village. Despite Derouin's assurances of friendship, the Otoes and Missourias received him cooly, and the trader's life was repeatedly threatened by one group of Otoe warriors. Other Otoes and Missourias interceded in his behalf, but the second group then demanded trade goods for their assistance and Derouin eventually was forced to give up most of his merchandise in return for his life.

Enraged over the tribesmen's actions, the Spaniards tried to punish the Otoes and Missourias by forbidding all traders to carry merchandise up the Missouri River. This measure proved disastrous for Spain because British traders, still active among the Iowas, willingly supplied guns and powder to the Indians along the Platte. In defiance, the Otoe-Missourias used their new firearms to launch a series of raids against the Kansas, a tribe still loyal to Spain.

The new weapons also enabled Otoe-Missouria warriors to defend their villages in a number of skirmishes with other tribes. Although they quar-

Courtesy Amon Carter Museum, Fort Worth, Texas

ARRIORS *INST-MUNTHA,* or "Iron Eagle," *Ko-Inga* or "Little Thunder," *Op-po-hom-mon-*, or "Buck Elk Walking," and *E'en-brick-to,* or "Blackbird." Trade blankets, shirts, welry, beads and guns contrast with tribal artisanry of moccasins, calumet, feather-work. uropean trade goods transformed Otoe-Missouria clothing, adornment and weaponry.

reled with the Pawnees, a more serious confrontation occurred between the Otoe-Missourias and the Omahas. In the winter of 1800-1801, smallpox spread up the Missouri, taking a heavy toll of many of the tribes. The Otoe-Missourias were spared serious losses but the Omahas lost many of their traditional leaders including Blackbird, a chief friendly to the Platte River tribes. The new Omaha leader, Big Rabbit, was anxious for war and led a surprise attack upon the Otoe-Missouria village. The Omahas set several lodges afire, attempting to ambush the Otoe and Missouria warriors as they rushed forward to their kinsmen's defense. Unfortunately for the Omahas, a storm swept in over the prairie, extinguishing the fires and soaking the raiders' powder. Although the Omahas stole several horses, the Otoe-Missourias rallied and drove the attackers across the Platte, inflicting heavy casualties upon the Omaha war party.

BIG KNIVES ON THE PLATTE

In 1804, as the Lewis and Clark expedition ascended the Missouri River, the American explorers dispatched two men overland to the Otoe-Missouria village with invitations for tribal leaders to meet with the expedition. Most of the Otoe-Missouria people were absent on their spring hunt, but during August a party of Otoes and Missourias met with the explorers who presented the Indians with gifts and informed them that the "*Mahehunjeh*" or "Big Knives" had replaced the Spanish at St. Louis. The Otoe-

Missouria reaction to such news remains unknown, but the warriors were friendly toward the Americans and supported Lewis and Clark's efforts to negotiate a peace between their people and the Omahas.

From the journals of the Lewis and Clark expedition and from diaries of other explorers, a good picture of the Otoe-Missouria people during the first decade of the nineteenth century emerges. At this time the two tribes were sharing a single village on the south side of the Platte about five miles upstream from the mouth of the Elkhorn River. Estimates of their numbers vary, but most white observers indicated that the Otoes could muster 125 warriors from a total population of approximately 500 people. The Missourias had eighty-five fighting men among a tribe of about 300 Indians. The village was led by two Otoe chiefs, Little Thief and Big Horse, and although the Otoe-Missouria people did not claim exclusive rights to the region, they hunted over a broad area stretching from western Iowa, along the Platte and Nemahaw Rivers, and out onto the Great Plains. American travelers were impressed with the richness of the Otoe-Missouria hunting lands, remarking that the region contained valuable lumber resources and was "extremely fertile and well watered." The area also abounded in game and white traders calculated that Otoe-Missouria hunters annually harvested furs valued at over six thousand dollars, including many beaver, otter, and raccoon pelts.

While meeting with Lewis and Clark, the Otoes

and Missourias accepted an invitation by the Americans for several of their chiefs to visit the "Great White Father" in Washington. During 1805, Otoe-Missouria chiefs made plans for the journey and in October they assembled with other Indians at St. Louis where government officials prepared to send the tribesmen east. Before the Indians could depart, however, several of the Otoes became ill and announced that they wished to return to their village. Federal agents agreed, but as the Otoes and Missourias retraced their voyage up the Missouri one of the Otoe chiefs died, causing the Americans to fear that the tribe would become alienated from the United States.

Much of the American concern over potential Otoe-Missouria hostility resulted from the deteriorating state of Indian-white relations east of the Mississippi. In the years following the Louisiana Purchase, the United States was hard pressed to control the warlike Kickapoos and Potawatomis in Illinois. American officials believed that British Indian agents were agitating the Illinois tribes and inasmuch as the Otoes had been receptive to British traders, the Americans feared that the Otoes and Missourias also might take up the hatchet against the United States.

American apprehension was unjustified, for the primary cause of Indian discontent lay in the advance of white settlement upon tribal hunting lands. The Shawnee Prophet, Tens-kwau-ta-waw, not the British, was responsible for inflaming the Indians against the United States as he attempted to forge a militant confederation of frontier tribes to halt white encroachment on tribal territories. Ironically, several factors combined to keep the Otoes and Missourias friendly to the Americans. Most important was geography. Not only were the Otoes and Missourias beyond the effective reach of the Shawnees at Prophetstown, they also lived beyond the American frontier. Although American farmers were over-running Indians lands in Ohio and Indiana, most white settlement had not crossed the Mississippi and the Otoe-Missourias continued to welcome American traders into their village. They also were unwilling to join any inter-tribal confederacy, which included such traditional Indian enemies as the Sacs and Foxes. The Missourias, particularly, could not forget the bloody ambush of 1796, and in 1808 Otoe and Missouria warriors had joined with the Omahas to attack a party of Sacs and Foxes who were threatening to settle on tribal hunting lands in western Iowa.

During the summer of 1812, a few young Otoe-Missouria warriors attended an inter-tribal council at a Sac village in eastern Iowa where envoys from the Shawnee Prophet attempted to enlist them into the anti-American confederacy. Although the young warriors agreed to take the Shawnee message back to their village, they refused to join the Prophet's cause. Their kinsmen on the Platte reacted in a similar manner, answering that there was more profit in trapping beaver than in fighting the Big

Knives. In 1814, the Walker, a Missouria chief, visited Governor William Clark in St. Louis, informing him that the Otoes and Missourias were allies of the United States and considered themselves to be under American protection.

Because the Otoe-Missouria people remained friendly throughout the War of 1812, they did not take part in any of the immediate post-war treaties, but in 1817 Big Horse led a delegation of Otoe and Missouria warriors to St. Louis where they joined with other Missouri River tribes to sign a series of agreements re-affirming their ties to the United States. Once again the Otoes and Missourias vowed their friendship to the Big Knives and promised to make no contacts with foreign powers, especially the British and Spanish.

The continuing pledges of Otoe-Missouria friendship reflected the growing economic dependence of the Indians upon American traders. Although a few British merchants still reached the Missouri River, their numbers steadily declined and the Otoe-Missouria people relied upon Americans such as Manuel Lisa and Pierre Chouteau to supply them with powder, lead, and blankets. In 1804, after Louisiana passed into American hands, government officials had abandoned the old Spanish restrictions and had opened the Indian trade to any frontiersman who could qualify for a trading license. Anxious for new markets, many traders had flocked to the Otoe-Missouria village and the tribesmen reaped advantages from the competition among the different merchants. The fur trade boomed until 1808 when government officials banned all traders from the upper Missouri in an attempt to punish the Osages, Kansas, Pawnees, and Omahas: tribes that had attacked American trading parties. Although the Otoes and Missourias did not participate in the attacks, they were forced to suffer with the guilty parties. When the War of 1812 erupted, however, federal officials encouraged the Missouri Fur Company to trade with friendly tribes. During the summer of that year, Manuel Lisa established a trading post in western Iowa, near the mouth of the Boyer River.

The Otoes and Missourias immediately began to trade with Lisa, journeying to his post and welcoming Missouri Fur Company employees into their village. Because many of the Pawnees were alienated from the Americans, the Otoes and Missourias served as middlemen, purchasing supplies from American merchants and selling the trade goods to the Pawnees at a profit. Eager to keep the American trade open, in 1815 Otoe warriors rescued one of Lisa's partners when the trader was attacked by a small party of pro-British Iowas near the mouth of the Platte River.

The Otoe-Iowa confrontation was indicative of the unsettled conditions among the Missouri River tribes in the second decade of the nineteenth century. During the War of 1812, Hard Heart, a prominent chief of the Iowas, opposed his tribesmen's war against the Americans and left his village, seeking exile among the Otoe-Missourias. Although the war ended in 1815, dissension continued to plague the Iowas and in 1819 about half of the tribe, almost 400 people, followed Hard Heart to the Otoe-Missouria village on the Platte. The Iowas remained among the Otoe-Missouria people for about one year, returning to the Des Moines River in 1821, but the intra-tribal quarreling which had troubled the Iowas now spread to the Platte River tribes.

The dispute involved prominent Otoe families and eventually split the tribe into two separate villages. In 1818, Cut Nose, kinsmen of Crenier, a respected Otoe leader, quarreled with the Brave, a brother of Big Horse. The feud simmered for three years, but in 1821, after a member of the Brave's family insulted Cut Nose's wife, the two warriors fought openly, each wounding the other mortally. Many of the Otoe and Missouria tribesmen took sides in the dispute, and in the aftermath the opposing factions divided, forming two villages about thirty miles apart in the lower Platte River Valley.

Anxious to restore stability among the Indians along the Missouri, in September, 1819, government officials negotiated a peace between the Otoe-Missourias and the Kansas, a tribe with whom the Otoes and Missourias had intermittently quarreled for several years. One month later, Otoe, Missouria, and Iowa chiefs also met with members of the Stephen H. Long Expedition near the site of Lisa's trading post in western Iowa. The Americans were pleased to see that the Iowas were living among the Otoe-Missourias and hoped that their association with the Platte tribes would make them more friendly toward the United States. Benjamin O'Fallon, the government spokesman, urged the Indians to cease all warfare and live in peace, warning the tribesmen that their disputes threatened the fur trade and brought hunger and suffering to their villages. The Otoe and Missouria chiefs responded favorably and the entire council took place amidst much dancing and celebration. Impressed by their warm reception, federal officials decided to establish a permanent military post in the region, and in 1820 Fort Atkinson was erected on the site of modern Council Bluffs. Indian agents believed the new post would bring peace to the Missouri River tribes and would keep Canadian traders from penetrating into the region.

Among the many Otoe and Missouria chiefs who attended the meeting near Council Bluffs was *Shaumonekusse* or "The Prairie Wolf," also known as *Iotan*. Already a famous warrior, *Iotan* dominated tribal affairs during the third and fourth decades of the nineteenth century, impressing white observers who described the Otoe leader in complimentary terms. A tall, muscular man, *Iotan* is portrayed as "well-proportioned," with piercing dark eyes and a "fine and intelligent cast of features." Many military officers considered him to be "one of the most intelligent Indians on the frontier," but commented that his stern appearance often was broken by a good-natured sense of humor.

In 1821, *Iotan,* his wife, Eagle of Delight, and several other Otoes and Missourias accompanied a delegation of Indians who toured cities along the eastern seaboard. On New Year's Eve, December 31, 1821, the tribesmen attended a reception at the White House where they mingled with President Monroe, Secretary of State Adams, and various foreign dignitaries. Attired in a headdress of scarlet horsehair and buffalo horns, *Iotan* presented an imposing appearance, but the slender Eagle of Delight was the center of attention, attracting admiring glances from both American and European officials. The Otoes remained on the east coast until March, 1822, when laden with presents, they returned to Nebraska.

The years following the eastern journey were not happy ones for *Iotan* and his wife. Shortly after returning to their village, Eagle of Delight contracted the measles and died. Grief stricken, *Iotan* killed three of his finest horses to carry Eagle of Delight's spirit to the northern afterworld. The Otoe warrior then tried to drown his sorrow in frontier whiskey but these efforts also led to disaster. Late in 1822, following an extended drinking bout, *Iotan* quarreled with his younger brother, Blue Eyes. In a fit of anger, *Iotan* killed his brother, then filled with remorse, he exiled himself from his people, living among the Pawnees for about two years.

While among the Pawnees, *Iotan* accompanied war parties out onto the plains, seeking death in encounters with the Sioux and Comanches. Yet his

Courtesy Western History Collections, University of Oklahoma Library

YNE HUDJIHINI, or "Eagle of Delight," wife of Chief *Iotan*, who charmed federal icials during a visit to Washington, D. C., in 1821-1822, but died from measles not long er she returned home.

medicine was strong and he counted many coups, taking several scalps and capturing numerous horses. Finally, by 1825 his grief was gone and he went back to the Otoe-Missourias.

Upon his return to the Platte, *Iotan's* stature as a chief increased rapidly. In September, 1825, the Otoes and Missourias met with government officials at Fort Atkinson, signing a new treaty of peace and friendship with the United States and promising to trade only with American merchants. The tribesmen also agreed to surrender all foreigners to American military officers and to give up all warriors committing depredations against American citizens. In return, the treaty commissioners assured the Indians that the government would pay for all damage to Otoe-Missouria property caused by white settlers. The four Otoe-Missouria chiefs who signed the treaty were Big Woman, Only Chief, Big Kaw, and *Iotan*.

Between 1825 and 1830, the two Otoe-Missouria villages reunited, forming a single town on the southwest bank of the Platte, a day's ride upstream from the mouth of the Saline. Faced with a growing number of problems, the Otoe-Missouria people turned to *Iotan* and by 1830 the famous warrior had emerged as the leading chief of the tribe. Although he shared his position of leadership with other chiefs such as Big Kaw and The Thief, *Iotan's* influence dominated tribal councils and directed the course of tribal politics. A shrewd politician, *Iotan* successfully played his rivals off against each other, keeping

Big Kaw and The Thief busy with minor tribal affairs.

Iotan's growing influence was based upon his ability as a warrior. During the 1820's, Sac and Fox lands in Illinois were being settled by white farmers and many of the Sacs and Foxes established new villages in central Iowa. From their towns on the Des Moines River, Sac and Fox warriors ranged westward, trespassing upon Otoe-Missouria hunting lands and ambushing Otoe and Missouria warriors. In 1820, a Sac war party burned part of the Otoe-Missouria village while the tribe was absent on its autumn buffalo hunt. Although a temporary peace was re-established during the following year, it failed to last. Meanwhile, the Sacs and Foxes extended their raids to the Sioux and Omahas, and by the mid-1820's the entire Missouri Valley was engulfed in warfare.

Eager to end the conflict, in 1825 government officials at Prairie du Chien, Wisconsin, negotiated a tenuous peace between the Sacs and Foxes and the Sioux, establishing temporary boundaries between the intruders and their enemies. Despite government efforts, the warfare between the Otoe-Missourias and the Sacs and Foxes continued, and in 1828 Indian Agent John Dougherty assembled chiefs from the warring tribes at Cantonment Leavenworth, persuading both sides to sign a peace agreement. The Otoes and Missourias assumed that their enemies would withdraw from western Iowa, but the Sac chief Keokuk used the armistice to warn the

Otoes, Missourias and Omahas to stay on the west side of the Missouri. Angered by the Sac threat, *Iotan* and other Otoe-Missouria leaders rebuked Keokuk, calling him a liar and defiantly assuring the Sac that Otoe and Missouria warriors would hunt in western Iowa whenever they pleased.

Realizing that the Leavenworth peace had failed, Indian agents hurried to negotiate a new, more permanent settlement to the Otoe-Sac confrontation. Inasmuch as the lands in western Iowa were the primary cause of friction, government officials decided to purchase the region, insuring the right of all tribes to hunt peacefully in the area. In July, 1830, *Iotan* led a delegation of Otoe and Missouria chiefs to Prairie du Chien where the tribesmen gave up their claims to western Iowa. They also agreed to relinquish claims to a small tract along the western bank of the Missouri, between the mouths of the Great and Little Nemaha Rivers, to be used as a reservation for Otoe and Missouria "Half-Breeds" and for mixed-bloods from the Iowas, Omahas, and eastern Sioux. In return for their claims to the land, the tribe received about $127,000 in money and trade goods and a ten year annuity of $3,000. Yet neither *Iotan*, Big Kaw, nor The Thief believed that their people had given up their right to hunt in western Iowa. The Otoe-Missouria chiefs assumed that they would continue to hunt on the government lands east of the Missouri, but that the United States would be obligated to keep the peace in the region.

Yet *Iotan* and the other Otoe-Missouria leaders

Courtesy Western History Collections, University of Oklahoma Library

'ON-MON-I-CASE (also spelled *Shaumonekusse),* or *Iotan,* a chief who visited the President, cretary of State, and other dignitaries in the national capitol in the early 1820's, and played eading role in tribal affairs until 1837 when he was killed by another Otoe-Missouria.

were wrong. Anxious to remove all Indians from Illinois and Indiana, federal officials began to resettle the Kickapoos and Potawatomis along the Missouri Valley. By 1833, several hundred Kickapoos had established villages near Fort Leavenworth and were ranging northward, hunting along the Great Nemahaw. Although the Otoes and Missourias were not camping in the region, Indian agents realized that the lands belonged to them and hoped to forestall any clashes between the Platte tribes and the Kickapoos. Accordingly, in September, 1833, Commissioner Henry Ellsworth and a party of government officials journeyed into the Otoe-Missouria village, intending to purchase the region west of the Half-Breed Reservation and between the Nemahaw Rivers.

Accompanying Ellsworth was the young journalist John Treat Irving, whose *Indian Sketches* remains one of the best accounts of *Iotan* and the Otoe-Missouria people. As the officials approached the village, they were greeted by *Iotan* who then signaled his warriors to charge forward to welcome the Americans. Honored, but half-frightened by the spectacle, Irving described the greeting as follows: "Suddenly a loud roar rose from behind the bluff, and a dark troop of wild horsemen burst around its base, and came pouring down upon us. There must have been several hundred of them. Every man was naked, but glaring with paint. They flooded onward, pealing out scream upon scream, brandishing their spears, and whirling their tom-a-hawks around their heads . . . They were close upon us; — another moment — and we were lost . . . At that moment, at a signal from *Iotan,* the wild horde separated, and whirled around, enveloped in a cloud of dust . . . These warriors were highly ornamented; paint of every hue was laid upon their bodies . . . Long strings of wampum hung from their neck and ears . . . Their heads were shaven, and covered with vermilion, and from the top of each hung the chivalrous scalp lock, generally adorned with an eagle's plume. As much care had been bestowed upon the horses as upon their riders, and . . . they moved forward with proud step, as if conscious of the haughty character of those who guided them, but this was as much owing to the horsemanship of the riders, as to the spirit of the animals themselves . . ."

The treaty negotiations began on September 20 and lasted for two days. Assembled in *Iotan's* lodge, the chiefs and warriors of the Otoes and Missourias listened favorably to the speeches and arguments of the Americans. Knowing that their tribe had depleted most of the game south of the Little Nemahaw, the Indians decided to cede the region to the United States. Moreover, they were short of powder and clothing and needed the presents that the white men had brought in wagons. On September 21 *Iotan* and several other chiefs signed the treaty ceding over one million acres to the American government. In return they received additional annuities, trade goods and other payments totaling about $40,000. A large but questionable bargain for the government: the price averaged less than five cents per acre.

Three years later, in 1836, the Otoes and Missourias also gave up their claims to the Platte Purchase, an area compromising the northwest corner of Missouri. Once again they were desperately short of food and signed the document in return for a small payment in food and clothing. Merchandise worth $2,250 was distributed to the Otoe and Missouria chiefs immediately after the treaty and 500 bushels of government corn was parcelled out to the tribe in 1837.

The growing food shortages in the Otoe-Missouria village reflected their loss of hunting lands in western Iowa. Although *Iotan* and the other chiefs believed that the 1830 treaty guaranteed the tribe's right to hunt east of the Missouri, during the mid-1830's the federal government began to resettle part of the Potawatomis in the Council Bluffs region and the new emigrants claimed the area as their own. Otoe and Missouria hunters still crossed into western Iowa, but their lives were endangered by the more numerous Potawatomis. Meanwhile, Potawatomi hunters rapidly depleted the game near Council Bluffs, and by 1838 they also were crossing the Missouri, ranging into eastern Nebraska where they killed deer in the heart of the Otoe-Missouria homeland. Although local Indian agents attempted to compensate the Otoes and Missourias for the loss of the hunting lands in Iowa, the Senate refused to ratify the treaty and by 1840 the Platte River war-

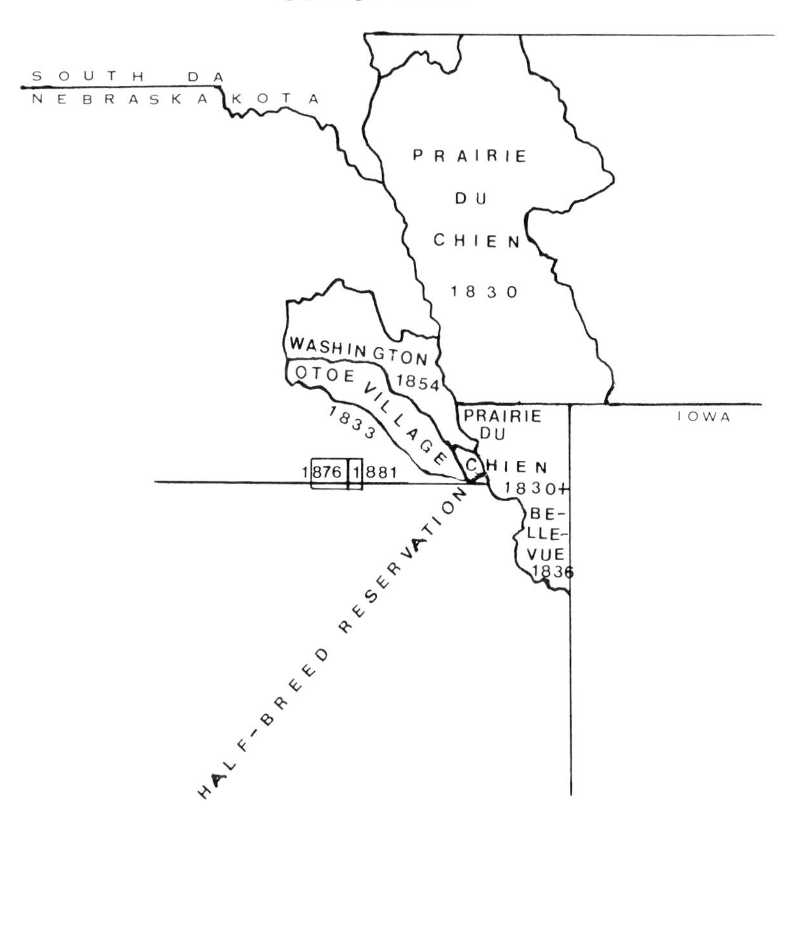

AP 2. *Map by Henry F. Dobyns*

riors were hard pressed to provide food for their families.

DARKNESS ON THE PRAIRIE

Food shortages were not the only problem that plagued the Otoe-Missouria people during the middle decades of the nineteenth century. In 1837 the proud *Iotan* was killed by another Otoe warrior in a dispute involving one of *Iotan's* wives. The chief's death split the Otoe-Missourias into quarreling factions, each threatening the lives of the others, and in 1839 most of the Missourias separated from the Otoes, forming a new village at the mouth of the Platte. Although Big Kaw and other chiefs tried to hold the tribe together, they failed, and by the mid-1840's the Otoe-Missouria people had divided into five small villages scattered along the Platte Valley from the Missouri River to the mouth of the Elkhorn.

Alcohol had played an important part in the quarrel resulting in *Iotan's* death and it continued to inundate the Platte River tribes. Both missionaries and Indian agents tried to stop the flow of frontier whiskey into the Otoe-Missouria villages, but they met with little success. Ignoring federal regulations, unscrupulous traders plied the Indians with the fiery liquid, first intoxicating the warriors then fleecing them out of their possessions. Inasmuch as the Otoe-Missouria lands no longer held large numbers of fur-bearing animals, many tribesmen, addicted to the whiskey, traded away their horses and weapons for kegs of the white man's poison. The whiskey trade not only left many Otoe-Missourias destitute, but the drunken brawls resulting from the traffic added to the internal quarrels among the tribes.

Among the few whites attempting to stop the whiskey trade was Moses Merrill, a Baptist missionary who in 1833 established a mission at Bellevue, across the Missouri from Council Bluffs. A dedicated evangelist, Merrill ministered to the Otoe-Missouria people until 1839, promoting agriculture and conducting a school for tribal children. Like many white men of his calling, Merrill measured both "Christianity" and "Progress" by white standards and continually was discouraged that the Otoe and Missouria warriors did not settle down on small acreages and become farmers. At first Big Kaw and the other chiefs half-heartedly supported the missionary's efforts, but when the mission cattle escaped and trampled their corn crop, they grew angry and questioned the white man's motives. Merrill paid for the corn, but the Otoes and Missourias expected the missionary to follow Indian patterns of hospitality and to share all of his food with hungry tribesmen. When Merrill refused, many of the Otoe and Missouria parents withdrew their children from the missionary's school.

The Otoe-Missouria attempts at farming reflected the deteriorating economic condition of the tribe during the 1840's. Because of the Potawatomis, they no longer could hunt across the Missouri in Iowa and their buffalo hunts on the plains were becoming less successful. Now short of horses and firearms, the Otoes and Missourias were forced to journey ever farther westward in search of the buffalo herds. Their ventures out onto the plains brought them in closer contact with the Sioux, who also hunted along the central Platte, attacking the Otoe and Missouria hunting parties. During the severe winter of 1842-43, many of the Indians were reduced to living on roots and other vegetable foods that they could gather in the river bottoms, resulting in the death of several old or weak tribesmen. In the following year they killed many buffalo but the herds were shrinking and by mid-century many of the Otoe and Missouria people had grown accustomed to empty cooking pots.

Facing starvation, Otoe and Missouri warriors sought food wherever it could be found, resulting in numerous clashes with their neighbors. In 1845, an Otoe-Missouria hunting party raided a Pawnee village while the Pawnees were absent on their winter hunt, seizing large caches of corn which the Pawnees had hidden among their lodges. During the next year they quarreled with the Omahas after the latter tribe moved one of their villages into the lower Platte Valley. Meanwhile, the Pawnees retaliated for the stolen corn, attacking a group of Otoes in central Nebraska, and in 1847 the Sioux again entered the warfare, ambushing a party of Otoe and Missouria warriors hunting buffalo west of Grand Island.

The conflict also spilled over onto the Americans. As their hunting lands shrank and more and more whites appeared along the Missouri, the Otoes and

Missourias lashed out at their former friends, blaming the Americans for the declining economic conditions in the lower Platte Valley. In 1839, they forced Merrill to abandon his mission and during the following year a small number of warriors crossed into Missouri where they slaughtered livestock to feed their hungry families. In the mid 1840's they often were forced to subsist on government rations, growing sullen over losing the dignity they formerly had held as self-sufficient hunters and warriors. Big Kaw's followers angrily fired at whites shipping on the Missouri but the chief defended his warriors, arguing that the harrassment was small payment for the government's broken promises in allowing the Potawatomis to settle on Otoe-Missouria hunting lands in western Iowa.

By 1850, most of the tribe realized that they no longer could remain in the Platte Valley. Big Kaw had died during the late 1840's and his successors, *Arkeketah* (Stand By It), Big Buffalo, and White Water informed government officials that the Otoe-Missouria people would reluctantly cede most of their lands in central Nebraska in exchange for a smaller reservation and increased government annuities. They had little choice. During the early 1850's, white emigrants flooded westward along the Platte as both gold seekers and Mormons journeyed toward their respective promised lands. The travelers either frightened away or killed the remaining game, imposing further hardships upon the Otoe-Missourias. Disease also took its toll. Both smallpox and cholera raged along the Missouri, further decimating the tribesmen and causing them to continually shift their villages. In desperate straits, many of the Otoe-Missourias were reduced to living in bark huts. Their constant relocation kept them from building the substantial earth lodges that once had comfortably housed them.

Pressured by white settlers anxious to move into Indian territory, the federal government took steps to clear the tribesmen's claims to lands in eastern Kansas and Nebraska. In 1853, Commissioner George Manypenny traveled among the frontier tribes, sampling red opinion regarding land cessions. The Otoes and Missourias informed him that they might cede their lands, but they wanted assurances that the new reservation would be located within their former territory. After returning to the east, Manypenny instructed Indian Agent James Gatewood to assemble a delegation of Otoe-Missouria leaders and accompany them to Washington where a treaty for the land cession would be negotiated. Yet Gatewood was anxious for the cession to take place and in February, 1854, without proper authority, he met with the Otoe-Missourias at one of their villages and negotiated a treaty on his own. Congratulating himself upon his supposed success, Gatewood then escorted the Otoe and Missouria leaders to Washington.

Although Manypenny and Secretary of Interior Robert McClelland were angry with Gatewood for his unauthorized treaty and later dismissed him from the Indian service, they signed a similar treaty with

Arkeketah, White Water, and the other Otoe-Missouria chiefs when the Indians arrived in the capital. On March 15, 1854, the Otoes and Missourias relinquished their claims to all lands west of the Missouri River except a reservation of about 162,000 acres stretching along the Kansas-Nebraska border and intersected by the Big Blue River. The tribesmen agreed to grant the government and certain railroads access across the reservation and to remove to the new tract within one year of the treaty date. They also gave up their right to hunt on lands in eastern Iowa. In return the United States promised to pay the Otoe-Missourias approximately $405,000 in cash and merchandise over the next forty years.

Half a decade later, during 1859-60, the federal government divided up the lands on the Half-Breed Reservation established by the treaty of 1830. Part of the land was distributed to the Otoe-Missouria mixed-bloods or to mixed-bloods from other tribes who were living in the region, and the remainder of the reservation was sold to whites. By accepting the "allotments" of lands within the former reservation, the Otoe-Missouria mixed-bloods supposedly severed their relationship with the tribe.

In July, 1855, the Otoe-Missouria people moved to their new reservation on the Kansas-Nebraska border. Well-watered by the Big Blue River, the area comprised some of the finest potential farmland in northern Kansas or southern Nebraska. The eastern third of the reservation was especially desirable because it contained groves of valuable hardwood, a commodity much in demand in the region. The Otoe-Missouria leaders had chosen well in deciding to relocate their people in this fertile valley, but the richness of the land attracted white attention, a circumstance that did not bode well for the Indians.

Attempting to convert the Otoe-Missouria people into agriculturists, Indian agents hired government farmers to work among the tribesmen, hoping that Otoe and Missouria warriors would learn from the farmers' example. The government also erected saw and grist mills, believing that such facilities would induce the Indians to adopt white ways.

The agents' efforts eventually produced some limited results. At the eastern end of the reservation several Otoe-Missouria families, most of mixed-blood origin, settled down and established small farms. Prominent among the mixed-blood community was the family of Francis Marion Barnes, a white settler married to Mary Jane Drips Benoist, a half-blood Otoe who formerly had received an allotment of the Half-Breed Reservation between the Nemahaw Rivers. Although most half-bloods who had owned allotments were no longer considered to be members of the tribe, the Barnes family was well received by the Otoe-Missouria chiefs and in 1871 a delegation of tribal leaders including Medicine Horse, Buffalo Chief, Missouria Chief and Pipestem wrote to the government acknowledging that the Indians considered Mrs. Barnes to be an Otoe-Missouria. Meanwhile Barnes erected a house, barn and other outbuildings upon reservation land, while

Courtesy Amon Carter Museum, Fort Worth, Texas

IEF *TCHA-WAN-NA-GA-HE*, known to English-speakers as "Buffalo Chief," showing a
ıplete change to European-style dress clothing. A Coyote Band leader on Big Blue
ervation, "Buffalo Chief" favored resettlement in Indian territory.

his wife opened a small trading post at modern Barneston.

The Barnes family received the support of Quaker Indian Agent A. L. Green who was assigned to the reservation in 1869 as part of President Grant's "Peace Policy." Green had no sooner arrived in Nebraska than he used all of his influence to block a recently negotiated treaty through which some Otoe-Missouria leaders had agreed to sell the reservation and move to Indian Territory. Charging that the agreement was an attempt by two railroad companies to cheat the Indians out of their lands, Green complained that "a few chiefs" had been "inveigled by corrupt and designing men" and that the proposed treaty did not represent the will of the Otoe-Missouria people. Green's allegations were supported by Commissioner of Indian Affairs Ely S. Parker and the treaty was not ratified.

Despite Green's contention that the treaty did not have the support of the Otoe-Missourias, his primary objection to the document was that it would have permitted the tribe to remove to Oklahoma. The Quaker opposed any plan allowing the Indians to move away from the "civilizing" influences of government Indian agents and enabling them to continue their traditional way of life. The immediate sale of the reservation was also protested by the Barnes family and by several of the mixed-bloods who wanted the eastern portion of the Otoe-Missouria lands allotted to themselves. After the Barnes family had sold its allotment on the old

Half-Breed Reservation, it now had no lands under its private ownership.

Disagreements over selling the reservation and moving to Oklahoma split the Otoe-Missouria people into two opposing factions. Those Indians who had begun to adopt white ways followed the leadership of the mixed-bloods were known as the "Quaker Band," because they subscribed to the acculturation program of the Quaker Indian agents. In contrast, the Otoe-Missourias who wished to continue in the old ways of their fathers were called the "Wild Otoes" or the "Coyote Band." Led by such traditional chiefs as *Arkeketah,* Medicine Horse, Buffalo Chief, and Pipestem, the Coyote Band was anxious to sell their reservation on the Big Blue and remove to Indian Territory where white influence would be minimized.

Although the split among the Otoe-Missouria people resulted from an honest difference of opinion, it was aggravated by white interests who became involved on both sides. The Indian agents supported the Quaker Band, but the Coyote Band received questionable encouragement from the large numbers of white settlers who crowded the lands bordering the reservation. The settlers cared little about the Coyote Band's desire to preserve their ancient way of life, but they were eager for the tribe to move to Oklahoma, hoping that the entire reservation would then be sold to the public. Neighboring farmers took advantage of the Coyote Band's anxiety to leave and persuaded several of the Coyote leaders that they had nothing to lose in selling their timber rights to the reservation. Although government Indian agents intervened, white lumbermen cut down and hauled away much valuable timber before troops from Fort Leavenworth drove the settlers off the reservation.

Reacting to public pressure, in 1872 Congress voted to survey and appraise the western half of the Otoe-Missouria lands, and with the Indians' permission, offer the tract for sale to nearby whites. Both factions among the Otoe-Missourias opposed the measure. The Quaker Band voted against accepting the legislation since it did not guarantee the allotment of lands on the eastern part of the reserve and the Coyote People refuted the act because it did not provide for the sale of the entire reservation and the removal of the tribe to Indian Territory.

Anxious to investigate the Otoe-Missouria motives for opposing legislation, the government invited a delegation of tribal chiefs to Washington. In 1873, when the Indians arrived in the capital they met with federal officials, who informed them that henceforward their annuities would no longer be distributed to the tribe but would be held by the Indian agents and paid out only to those Indians who were working at jobs approved by the agents. The chief objected that the government action was fraudulent and forced the Otoes and Missourias to labor for money already guaranteed to them by treaty, but their protests fell upon deaf ears.

Unable to change the government's decision, the chiefs returned to the reservation where the Coyote

Courtesy Western History Collections, University of Oklahoma Library

-*T-NEW-WAY,* or "Little Pipe" led part of the Coyote Band during its flight from the Big ue Reservation during 1876. He was later imprisoned at Fort Hays, Kansas. In this rtrait, he wears a wealth of trade beads and holds a fancy tomahawk, yet maintained some bal dress patterns of ceremonial significance.

Band received the news angrily, threatening to seize their money and spend it as they liked. Their discontent smoldered throughout the winter of 1873-74, but in the following summer, after drought and grasshoppers had destroyed most of their corn crop, about ninety members of the Coyote Band led by Medicine Horse and Little Pipe bolted the reservation and fled toward southwestern Kansas, intending to hunt buffalo on the plains. The fugitives were intercepted by federal troops from Fort Hays and returned to the reservation, but Medicine Horse, Little Pipe and four other warriors were temporarily imprisoned. Although the Otoe-Missouria leaders finally were released, the government deducted nearly $1,000 from tribal annuities to pay the army for its efforts.

Yet the flight of the Coyote Band off the reservation convinced government officials that the Otoe-Missourias were discontented with the lands on the Big Blue and were eager to go to Indian Territory. In 1876, government officials again made plans to survey and sell the western part of the reservation. Although they still preferred to sell all their lands, this time the Coyote People agreed to the government plans, envisioning the sale as the first step toward removal. The Quaker Band also supported the measure, being afraid that if the legislation failed, white Nebraskans might pressure Congress into abolishing all Otoe-Missouria lands in Kansas and Nebraska.

The actual sale of the reservation lands reflected

the growing influence of western politicians in Washington. After a group of three commissioners appraised the region, the lands were offered for sale only to white farmers who already had settled upon them. Such a condition was questionable since it kept the price of the lands very low, effectively barring large speculators from the bidding. Moreover, the occupancy regulation literally encouraged whites to trespass upon Indian lands because only illegal white squatters could purchase them. To make matters worse, proceeds from the land sales were to be distributed to the Indians but many of the whites settled on the reservation refused to make the payments because under the terms of the legislation, the lands could not be sold to anyone else. Government officials offered the tracts of lands for sale through the Beatrice, Nebraska land office during 1877, but one year later, in his annual report, Indian Agent Jesse Griest admitted that the land sales had been disastrous. Although the western half of the Big Blue Reservation was now overrun with whites, the Otoe-Missouria people still had received almost no money from the squatters.

With conditions deteriorating, by 1878 even most members of the Quaker Band agreed that the Otoe-Missouria people could no longer remain in Kansas and Nebraska. Emboldened by the recent land sales, white settlers now crossed over into the eastern portion of the reservation, trespassing on tribal lands farmed by mixed-bloods and other supporters of the Quaker Band. The constant harassment by whites kept Quaker Band farmers from their fields and convinced them that the Coyote People had been right in wanting to move to Indian Territory.

Yet the division that had plagued the tribe in the past continued, for now the Coyote Band and Quaker Band disagreed over what lands in Indian Territory should be their new home. In 1878, a party of Coyote Band leaders traveled to the Indian Territory where they selected an area just west of the Sac and Fox Agency, on the Cimarron River in central Oklahoma. The region was rich in game but the Quaker Band preferred to settle in farming country in the northern part of the territory, near the Pawnees, Poncas, and Osages. Although government officials also argued for the northern location, in January, 1880, four families from the Coyote Band left Nebraska and erected new lodges along the Cimarron. During the following summer about 180 other members of the Coyote Band joined them.

While the Coyote Band was establishing a new village in central Oklahoma, several spokesmen for the Quaker Band traveled to Washington where they used their influence to secure a reservation near the Poncas and Pawnees. In March, 1881, after the delegation returned to Nebraska, Congress provided for the sale of the remaining Otoe-Missouria lands on the Big Blue and the removal of the tribe into Indian Territory. During the following two months, members of the Quaker Band journeyed into modern Oklahoma where they chose lands along Red Rock

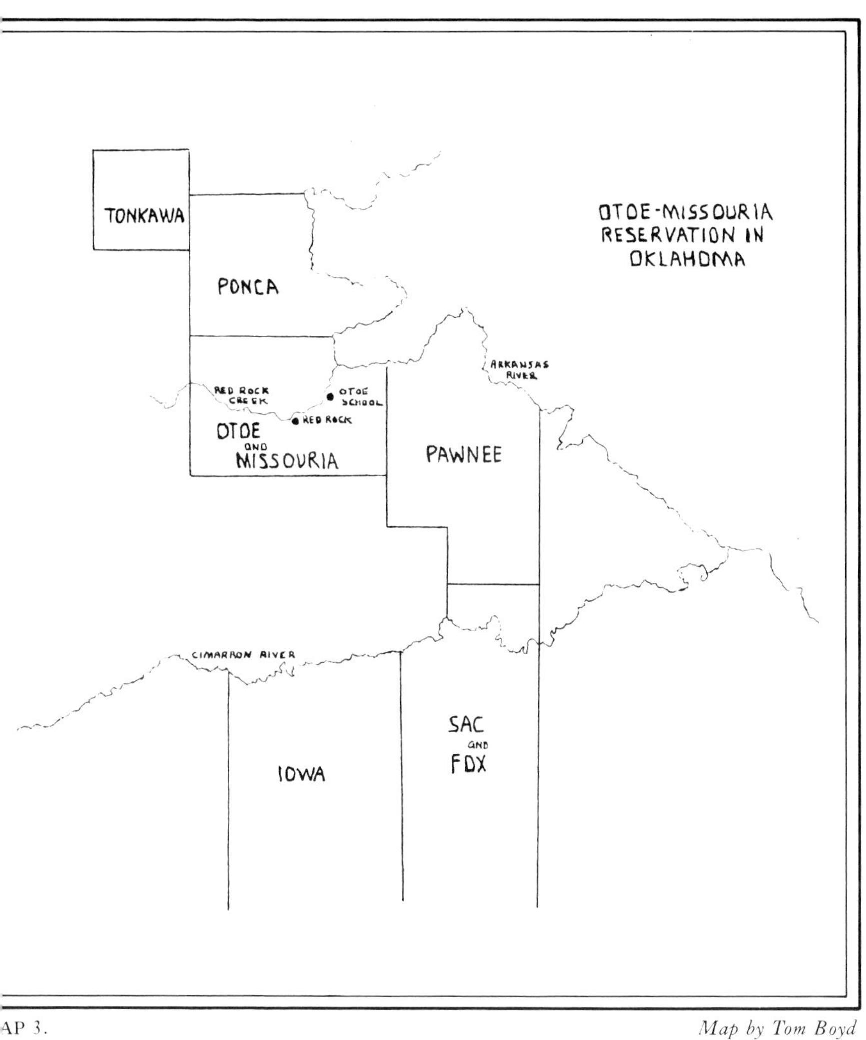

AP 3. *Map by Tom Boyd*

Creek, just south of the Ponca Reservation. Although the Otoes and Missourias already settled on the Cimarron protested against the choice, the government agreed with the Quaker Band and established the Otoe-Missouria reservation on Red Rock Creek in north-central Oklahoma.

Once the lands had been selected, most members of the Quaker Band were anxious to leave for their new home. When news of the Otoe-Missourias' pending removal reached whites in Kansas and Nebraska, more squatters crowded onto tribal lands east of the Big Blue. Angry over the encroachment, the Quaker Band urged their agents to speed up the removal process and by autumn arrangements were complete. On October 5, 1881, over 230 Otoes and Missourias left Nebraska for their new reservation along Red Rock Creek. Their household goods and other possessions were carried in seventy wagons and the Indian horse herd followed behind. After over two weeks on the trail, the tribesmen arrived at Red Rock on October 23, 1881.

As most of the Quaker Band settled into their new home, federal officials took measures to sell the remaining tribal lands on the Big Blue River. Many Otoes and Missourias held serious doubts about the sale since they had not yet received adequate payment for the western portion of the reservation supposedly purchased by whites in 1876-1877. Reacting to the influence of frontier politicians, land office bureaucrats had allowed settlers purchasing tracts of land within the western part of the Big Blue Reservation to defer their payments for an indefinite period. Although Indian agents assured the Otoe-Missourias they would receive interest on the overdue funds, the Indians did not want to sell the remainder of the reservation under such circumstances.

Foremost among these concerned about the sale of the eastern portion of the Big Blue lands was the Barnes family. Throughout the 1870's Mary Barnes had petitioned various officials, asking that her family and other acculturated tribe members be given allotments of land on the eastern side of the reservation. In 1881, when Congress provided for the sale of the remaining Otoe-Missouria lands in Kansas and Nebraska, federal agents agreed to withhold nine 160 acre tracts upon which the Barnes family and other Indians had erected buildings or other improvements. Although the government held the nine tracts in trust, the Indians would be allowed to remain on the lands. If they continued to reside on the farms through 1894, the lands would be theirs.

Meanwhile, the sale of other reservation lands proceeded according to government, but not Otoe-Missouria, plans. Once again federal officials offered the tracts of reservation lands at auction, and once again the Indians were victimized by highly organized, but unscrupulous whites. The tribesmen were to receive the proceeds from the sale, but many of the settlers bidding on the lands formed an organization to keep the bids low. Others defaulted from paying the full amount when the tracts brought a high price, knowing that the government would be forced to offer the repossessed lands for sale at a second time. At the second sale they then purchased the farms at a fraction of their official price per acre. To add to the confusion, federal officials again allowed the settlers to defer part of their payments and, in some instances, those whites who had purchased lands on the eastern portion of the Big Blue Reservation had still failed to pay for the tracts seventeen years after the lands supposedly had been sold. Finally, in 1899, under pressure from white officials, most of the Otoe-Missouria people agreed to accept a reduced payment for their lands in Kansas and Nebraska. Desperately short of money and afraid that they might receive nothing, the tribe accepted a final payment of about $120,000. The total figure still owed to them including interest, was more than $270,000.

Charges of fraud and collusion resulting from the actual land sales brought a federal investigation, and to his discredit, Francis M. Barnes was implicated. Attempting to purchase other tracts to add to his family allotment, in 1885, Barnes was convicted of conspiring with certain settlers in an illegal price-fixing scheme designed to lower the cost of reservation lands bought at auction. He paid a fine of $365.

A NEW HOME IN OKLAHOMA

Embittered over the location of the new reservation, many members of the Coyote Band refused to join with their kinsmen at Red Rock. Led by old Medicine Horse, over two hundred of the Coyote people remained on the Cimarron, planting small gardens and hunting in the surrounding region. In 1883, the area became part of the Iowa reservation, but the Iowas befriended Medicine Horse's followers, sharing food and other supplies with them. Yet family ties among the Otoe-Missouria people remained strong and, during the last half of the 1880's, many of the Coyote Band left the Cimarron and joined their relatives on the Otoe-Missouria reservation. By 1886, only 125 Coyote people still lived among the Iowas and three years later their number had shrunk to seventy-five. In 1890, after the Iowa reservation was allotted, almost all the remaining members of the Coyote Band moved to Red Rock.

Despite their diminishing numbers, the conservatism of the Coyote Band still exerted a strong influence within the tribe. Many Otoe-Missourias continued to cling to the ways of their fathers, preferring the communal ownership of land and certain other property to the individualism of their white neighbors. Although most of the tribesmen now dressed in white man's garments, some of the older people still felt more comfortable in the traditional clothing of their ancestors. By 1890, the majority of the Otoe-Missouria people were bilingual, speaking both English and their native language, but most adults still used the tongue of their forefathers in communicating with other members of the tribe. Indian agents and other white officials attempted to discourage many of the tribal ceremonies, yet these observances also persisted. A sociable people, the Otoe-Missourias had no intentions of giving up their traditional dances and celebrations.

Yet important changes did take place within Otoe-Missouria society. Most prominent among those things ushering in a new way of life was the Otoe-Missouria Boarding School. The institution was originally established by Quakers on the Big Blue reservation but when the Indians removed to Oklahoma the teachers and school equipment accompanied them. At Red Rock a new frame school building was erected and by 1882 classes again were in session. The school's curriculum reflected a mixture of white social and academic standards. In addition to such basics as reading, writing, and arithmetic, Otoe-Missouria students learned a variety of vocational subjects. Boys were taught carpentry or agriculture while their sisters learned how to cook, sew, or clean house. The young Indian students also were indoctrinated with white cultural values. To the teachers' discredit, they often taught that everything Indian was undesirable, urging the students to exchange their tribal ways for those of the white man.

Enrollment at the school varied from year to year, but after 1895 over seventy students usually were in attendance. Although part of the children lived at home, many of the students stayed in the school dormitories. The school buildings burned twice, in 1902 and 1907, but after each fire new structures were erected. Ironically, the school's success in introducing white values among the tribe eventually contributed to the institution's closure. By 1918,

Courtesy Amon Carter Museum, Fort Worth, Texas

UFFALO CHIEF" in a European-style dress suit; Chief Medicine Horse wearing more ditional tribal garb, but wearing numerous trade beads and holding a tomahawk; and erpreter Baptiste Barnaby (right).

most of the tribal funds were siphoned off in per capita payments and many Otoe-Missouria parents preferred to send their children to public schools in neighboring white communities. On June 30, 1918, the school closed permanently. Several of the school buildings later were used as part of the Otoe-Missouria Tribal Center.

The Indians adapted to white society in other ways. By 1890, the Otoe-Missourias had established their own reservation court system which adjudicated both criminal and civil cases among their people. Several respected and capable leaders, including White Horse, *Wayhonaryea,* and Joe John served as judges. The courts were assisted by a reservation police force comprised of about half a dozen Otoe-Missouria policemen.

After 1895 growing numbers of tribesmen adopted white farming methods. Although they still held their lands communally, Otoe-Missouria farmers tended individual fields, planting crops of wheat, corn, oats, and potatoes. Many of the farms were enclosed by fences and some of the farmers lived in substantial farm houses surrounded by numerous outbuildings and carefully nurtured orchards. A few of the Otoe-Missouria farmers owned handsome teams of horses or mules and some even accepted hauling contracts from white businessmen in the region.

Despite the "progress" down the white man's road, many Otoe-Missourias remained reluctant to accept all of the white values. Most notable was the

Courtesy Western History Collections, University of Oklahoma Library

'OE-MISSOURIA INDIAN POLICEMEN on the Red Rock Reservation, mounted and in at st semi-uniform of the U. S. Bureau of Indian Affairs Indian Police. They cooperated th a tribal court system to maintain law and order.

tribe's steadfast opposition to the allotment of tribal lands into small individual homesteads. Hoping to accelerate the assimilation of Indians into the American mainstream, Congress in 1887 passed the Dawes Act, legislation designed to end the reservation system. Upon the President's discretion, the government was empowered to divide up many of the reservations, parcelling out tribal lands in small allotments which were assigned to individual Indians. Although the tribesmen were expected to live upon and farm their allotments, the government planned to hold the land in trust for twenty-five years, after which the title to the acreages would be given to the individual Indians. Upon receiving title to his lands, the Indian would become a citizen of the United States and of the state or territory in which he lived. Surplus reservation lands not allotted to the tribesmen would then be sold to whites.

Anxious for the allotment of Otoe-Missouria lands, in 1890 Indian Agent D. J. M. Wood wrote to his superiors suggesting that reservation lands near Red Rock be divided among all those tribesmen who would accept them. In response, during October, 1890, President Benjamin Harrison appointed Helen P. Clarke, an acculturated half-blood Blackfoot woman from Montana as special allotting agent for the Otoe-Missourias, Pawnees, Poncas, and Tonkawas. Clarke was instructed to survey and allot the Otoe-Missourias reservation. She arrived at Red Rock on July 1, 1891.

Although Wood belatedly warned Miss Clarke

that "some of the Otoes are opposed to allotments," the allotting agent forged ahead, journeying about the reservation in preparation for her survey. Still a warriors society, the Otoe-Missourias were angry that the government had sent a woman to allot their lands. Led by James Whitewater, George Arkeketah and William Faw-Faw, many of the Otoe-Missouria people harassed the surveyors, pulling up their markers and pilfering their equipment. Other Otoe-Missourias threatened to kill the first member of their tribe who dared accept an allotment. By September Miss Clarke had made little progress and complained to Commissioner of Indian Affiars Thomas J. Morgan that the stubborn resistance of the Otoe-Missourias had now encouraged both the Poncas and the Pawnees to also oppose the allotment system.

Clarke left the Otoe-Missouria reservation early in December, reporting that she had convinced 122 of about 350 tribe members to accept the allotments. The agent's claim was far too optimistic. Anxious to be rid of the bureaucrat, many Otoe-Missourias had agreed to the allotment system only as a ruse to get Clarke off the reservation. With the agent gone, the tribesmen returned to their former position, again refusing to accept the small acreages.

Angered over the Indians' refusal, some officials blamed the influence of nearby ranchers who leased part of the reservation from the tribe and who also opposed allotments in the hope of continuing to graze their cattle on Indian lands. Such accusations only masked the government's inability to understand the Otoe-Missourias' sincere dislike of the allotment system. In 1892, another agent, James G. Hatchitt, was ordered to assist Miss Clarke and during the next two years both officials scoured the reservation, using all their powers to persuade the Indians to accept the small acreages. Finally, during the summer of 1894, about half of the tribe (175 Otoe-Missourias) reluctantly agreed to receive allotments. Afraid that the agents would *assign* them farms if they still refused to cooperate, these Otoe-Missourias gave in to the government's terms, hoping to at least choose the lands they wanted.

The government soon proved that the Otoe-Missouria fears were justified. In October, 1894, federal agents began to assign allotments to those tribesmen who had refused to specify which lands they wanted. By the following April, 362 Indians had either chosen or been given allotments, and 720 acres had been reserved for the agency, school, and other purposes. Government officials planned to sell the remaining Otoe-Missouria lands (almost 82,000 acres) and give the proceeds to the tribesmen.

Yet many of the Otoe-Missouria people still were not willing to accept the allotments. In April, 1895, before the final allotment schedule could be approved in Washington, a delegation of Otoe-Missouria leaders traveled to the capital where they registered a strong protest against the disolution of their reservation. Consisting of *Parthainga,* William Faw-Faw, Clem Jones, White Mule, Albert Green, James

Courtesy Western History Collections, University of Oklahoma Library

GROUP OF DISTINGUISHED LATE 19TH CENTURY OTOE-MISSOURIA TRIBAL LEADERS
ft to right) Hohe Deant, Albert Green, John Pipestem, Dave Pettit, William Faw-Faw,
rey Stone, Felix Robedeaux, and Sam Black. A group photographed in the 1890's when
ese leaders opposed land allotment. William Faw-Faw led the harassment of federal sur-
yors.

Whitewater, James Cleghorn and Mitchell Deroin, the party argued that their people had bought the reservation with tribal funds and should not be forced to sell the lands against their will. Speaking for the delegation, Deroin admitted that his people no longer could live by hunting and now were willing to "turn the soil and build houses" like white men, but they still wished to hold the reservation in common. The Otoe leader informed officials, "While we hold the land as it is, we can go anywhere and know that we have a home to come back to; but if we take allotments we will not have a home." Ending his speech, Deroin assured the white men that the Otoe-Missourias were anxious to preserve the reservation for their children.

Unfortunately for the Indians, Deroin's plea made little impact upon the bureaucrats. Acting Commissioner of Indian Affairs Thomas P. Smith replied that the government was convinced that allotment would benefit the Otoe-Missourias and that their reservation would be divided. Chiding the tribesmen, he informed them that their desire to hold the lands in common was unmanly and would deprive the tribe of its independence. Disappointed, the Otoe-Missourias returned to Red Rock.

Despite government efforts the Indians continued to send protests to Washington and many tribesmen refused to live on their allotments. In a last effort to settle the grievances, Helen Clarke returned to the reservation during 1898 and attempted to select new allotments for those tribesmen who were unhappy with their previous assignments. In 1898, she submitted a new schedule totaling 441 allotments comprising about 65,000 acres. Approximately 63,400 acres remained unallotted and unreserved. On December 7, 1899, Acting Secretary of the Interior Thomas Ryan approved the allotments and the reservation was divided.

Yet the fate of the unallotted reservations lands still remained in question. On many reservations such lands were sold to whites and the proceeds turned over to the Indians. In contrast, the Otoe-Missourias waged an active campaign attempting to retain control of the unallotted acreages. For once the government responded favorably and in 1904 Congress authorized the Interior Department to divide the remaining lands among tribe members, distributing the surplus so that each Indian received an equal number of acres. During the next two years a new census was taken and the surplus lands were surveyed and allotted. By 1907, 514 Otoe-Missourias held allotments of about 280 acres apiece.

According to the original Dawes Act, the government would hold all allotted lands "in trust" for twenty-five years after the reservation had been divided. During this period the tribesmen would pay no taxes on the acreages, but neither could they sell the plots. In 1906, however, Congress passed the Burke Act authorizing the Secretary of the Interior to terminate the trust period at any time he believed that an individual Indian was capable of managing his own affairs. Of course such a provision also permitted the tribesmen to sell his allotment. By 1909, a few Otoe-Missouria mixed-bloods, including the Barnes family, had persuaded the government to end the trust period on their allotments and had assumed complete control over their lands. Most of these tribesmen quickly sold the plots to white ranchers.

The government's trust period on other Otoe-Missouria lands ended under questionable circumstances. In 1912, oil was discovered in the Red Rock region and during the next several years many of the tribesmen leased the mineral rights to their allotments, often receiving handsome rents and royalties. White businessmen were anxious to gain control of the valuable oil lands and encouraged the Indians to ask for an end to their trust period, offering to buy the allotments at high prices. At first government agents refused to honor the Otoe-Missouria requests, asserting that the true value of the allotments remained uncertain and advising the Indians to continue leasing their lands. Yet in 1916 a government investigation found that certain officials at the Otoe Agency cooperated with a few businessmen in neighboring communities to swindle many of the Indians out of their allotments. By luring the tribesmen into debt and then securing a mortgage on their allotment, unscrupulous white entrepreneurs gained control of many of the acreages soon after they were released to the Indians.

Federal officials pressured other Otoe-Missourias to assume complete control over their allotments

Courtesy Western History Collections, University of Oklahoma Library

'HITE HORSE" wearing a full dress winter costume reflecting an amalgam of Great Plains d Great Lakes elements, rich in embroidery and beadwork, and topped by a Presidential ace Medal. "White Horse" carried a ceremonial eagle-wing at a tribal gathering near Red ock. He opposed land allotment.

before the twenty-five year trust period had ended. In a final attempt to force "independence" upon the tribesmen, between 1917 and 1921 a commission of Indian agents visited the Otoe-Missouria people in their homes, attempting to persuade the Indians to apply for a termination of the trust period. Many Otoe-Missourias refused, but the commission then arbitrarily declared them "competent" and presented them with a patent giving them complete control over their allotments. Afraid that they might lose their lands if they resisted, part of the tribesmen reluctantly accepted the patents. Others rejected the documents, claiming that the government still was obligated to hold the lands in trust until the twenty-five year period had ended. Finally, in 1921, the government reversed its policy, declaring that no more patents were to be forced upon the Indians. By that time, however, the allotments had been entered on state and local tax rolls and over ninety percent of the lands eventually passed from Indian hands. Ironically, at the request of the Otoe-Missouria people, government officials in 1922 renewed the trust period on the remaining lands for another ten year period.

A PEOPLE OF TWO CULTURES

In many ways the quarter century between 1899 and 1922 marked a low point in Otoe-Missouria history. Then in the years that followed conditions among the tribesmen improved. Over two dozen Otoe-Missourias served with American armed forces during World War I and their return to the Red Rock community brought back an infusion of new ideas and practices. Following Mitchell Deroin's 1895 prediction, more of the Indians began to farm their allotments while others raised small herds of cattle. Otoe-Missouria enrollments in neighboring schools increased, although many parents still preferred to send their children to Indian schools at Chilocco or Pawnee. Growing numbers of tribesmen professed Christianity, joining a wide variety of local churches, both Catholic and Protestant. Other Indians sought religious expression through the Native American Church, mingling traditional Otoe-Missouria beliefs with those of other tribes.

Although the old government by the clans had declined, it was replaced by a tribal council which exercised a growing influence over Otoe-Missouria affairs. Elected by adult tribe members, the council functioned without a written constitution but submitted the minutes of its meetings to the Office of Indian Affairs. Council meetings focused upon such problems as Otoe-Missouria claims against the government or the leasing of tribal lands, but all decisions usually were approved by a general meeting of the tribe before they became final.

Like other Oklahomans, the Otoe-Missouria people suffered during the dark years of the Great Depression. Many who had farmed their allotments abandoned such efforts as the dust storms of the 1930's swept through the Red Rock region. Leasing their lands to nearby ranchers, part of the tribesmen left their rural homes and moved to Tulsa or Oklahoma City. Others followed white Oklahomans to California, seeking employment on the farms and factories of the west coast. Some Otoe-Missouria men participated in the Civilian Conservation Corps or worked on Works Progress Administration projects throughout Oklahoma.

Although the Indian Reorganization Act of 1934 excluded the Otoes and Missourias, in 1935 the tribesmen successfully petitioned the government to have the federal trust period over their lands extended. One year later, after the passage of the Oklahoma Indian General Welfare Act several members of the tribe attempted to reorganize an Otoe-Missouria tribal government, proposing that a written constitution and bylaws be adopted. They met with little success. Most of the Indians were content with the old tribal council and had little interest in the more formal structure assumed by other tribes.

During World War II many modern Otoe-Missouria warriors fought in both the European and Pacific theatres. Since 1945 other members of the tribe have served their country in Korea and Vietnam. Today these veterans are honored by a memorial at the tribal center and at various dances and ceremonies. The Otoe-Missouria cemetery near Red Rock bears mute testimony to the sacrifices made by other tribesmen during these conflicts.

In the years that followed World War II, many returning Otoe-Missouria veterans were anxious to secure funds to make improvements on their farms and allotments. During 1948, eighteen tribesmen including Charles Robedeaux, Joe La Due and Joseph Young formed the Otoe Indian Credit Association, receiving funds from the Department of the Interior which they were authorized to loan to tribe members at low rates of interest. In the early 1950's many Otoe-Missourias borrowed money from the association but the program achieved only limited success. Unlike commercial banks, the tribal corporation loaned money to individuals who needed financial assistance, but who had limited or no collateral. Some of the tribesmen succeeded and promptly repaid their loans with interest. Others failed and were forced to default upon their promissary notes. Unfortunately, many of the Indians attempted to establish small farms during an age of large scale agriculture. Like many small white farmers, they had little chance of success.

If some Otoe-Missourias failed in their attempts at agriculture, the tribe achieved major victories in their claims against the United States. Admitting that much Indian land had been acquired under questionable circumstances, in 1946 the federal government established the Indian Claims Commission to "grant the Indian his long-delayed day in court." The commission was authorized to investigate Indian claims against the government and to provide a financial compensation to those tribes who had not received a fair price when their lands had been purchased by the government.

Eager to press their claims, the Otoe-Missouria tribal council employed the legal services of several attorneys, including Luther Bohanon, Bert Barefoot, Jr., and Bat Shunatona, an Otoe-Pawnee who was the first full-blood Indian graduate of the University of Oklahoma Law School. In 1947, the tribe presented a series of nine claims against the government asking for adequate compensation for their lands in Kansas and Nebraska. Tribal lawyers argued that the government owed the Otoe-Missouria people a sum in excess of ten million dollars. Hearings on the claims began at Red Rock in 1948 and continued intermittently for five years. Many Otoe-Missourias, including Ralph Dent, Moses Harragarra, Truman Dailey, and Felix Pipestem played major roles in the proceedings.

On March 31, 1953, the Indian Claims Commission members issued their opinion. Although the commission upheld the sale of the Big Blue reservation lands and ruled that the 1899 compromise over payment was valid, other decisions were in the Otoe-Missourias' favor. In examining the 1833 treaty, the commission decided that the amount paid the Indians for their lands between the Nemaha Rivers was "unconscionable" and awarded the tribe over $550,000 as compensation. The commissioners also investigated the 1854 treaty signed in Washington by *Arkeketah*, White Water, and other chiefs. Again ruling in the Indians' behalf, the claims commission charged that the federal government owed the Otoe-Missouria people approximately $625,000 for former tribal lands in east-central Nebraska.

Landmark decisions, the Otoe-Missouria judgements were the first in which the commissioners awarded additional compensation to a tribe for lands held by Indian title: lands occupied by the tribe for many years, but held without white documents such as treaties, deeds, etc. The government appealed the commission's verdict, carrying the case to the Supreme Court, but in October, 1955, the court upheld the decision and the government was ordered to pay the Otoe-Missouria people.

On May 19, 1956, Congress appropriated $1,156,000 (the total of both judgements) for the payment. After a vigorous argument among the Otoe-Missourias over whom should be eligible to share in the funds, a new tribal roll was established. Four years later, in 1960, almost two thousand persons of Otoe-Missouria descent shared in the appropriation. The per capita payment was $581.40.

Yet the 1960 payment was not the final compensation that the federal government awarded to the Otoe-Missouria people. The claims commission earlier had ruled that the Otoe-Missourias were not entitled to further payments for their 1830 cession of lands in western Iowa, but in the mid-1950's the commission reconsidered its opinion. As the Sacs and Foxes pressed their claims before the commissioners, new evidence emerged indicating that Otoe-Missouria warriors had hunted extensively over northwestern Missouri and southwestern Iowa, especially in the region between the Nodaway and

Boyer Rivers. Armed with this information, tribal attorneys again pressed the Otoe-Missouria claim to the area. In November, 1957, the claims commission reversed its former ruling and declared that the Otoe-Missourias had shared the region with three other tribes: the Omahas, Iowas, and Sacs and Foxes, and that each of the tribes was entitled to one fourth of the compensation to be awarded for the entire area. After consulting with their attorneys and sending a delegation of tribal leaders to Washington, the Otoe-Missouria people agreed to accept a compromise settlement of $175,000. In 1964, the money finally was appropriated, engendering a lengthy debate among tribe members over how the funds should be used. Some Otoe-Missourias, including Richard Kihega and Kenneth Black urged their kinsmen to invest the money in a tribal project. Others argued for another per capita payment. In a close vote the latter won and the Otoe-Missouria people again divided the money among themselves.

The decision to accept the per capita payment reflected the uncertainty of many tribesmen about the viability of a tribal economic project. Since 1964 much of that uncertainty has diminished. Although many tribesmen are employed, working on farms or in nearby communities, economic opportunity in the Red Rock region is limited. Anxious to provide their people with increased employment, in 1974 the tribal council initiated a plan for economic development.

Much of the council's program is based upon the

tribe's desire to retain and increase the tribal lands in the Red Rock region. As the 1975 Otoe-Missouria "Annual Report" points out, "The original Otoe-Missouria Indian reservation in Oklahoma contained 129,113.20 acres of tribally owned land. In less than one hundred years since the Otoe-Missouria Tribe arrived in Oklahoma and only sixty-nine years since the allotment process of the Otoe-Missouria Indian reservation was completed in 1906, the total land holdings of both the Otoe-Missouria Tribe and individual tribal members has dwindled to less than 29,000 acres. Believing that "Indian land is synonymous with tribal existence," the tribal council, under the aggressive leadership of Kenneth Black and Browning S. Pipestem has attempted to increase the Otoe-Missouria land base. During 1975 the Otoe-Missourias became the first Oklahoma tribe to secure a Farmer's Home Administration loan enabling them to purchase 280 acres of grazing land to add to their tribal holdings. Total tribal lands currently include 1680 acres, but plans have been made to buy another forty acre plot and to purchase additional acreages when they become available.

Yet land acquisition is only part of the tribe's economic plan. Through the efforts of the tribal council, the Otoe-Missouria people recently have received over $105,000 in government funds to partially finance a series of programs designed to benefit tribe members. A grant from the Office of Native American Programs, Department of Health, Education and Welfare provides the tribe with salaries for an Executive Director, other administrators, and secretarial assistance. The grant also enabled the Otoe-Missourias to purchase modern office equipment for the tribal center near Red Rock. Funds from the Tribal Government Development Program are being used to establish a training program for tribal officials and to implement a modern bookkeeping system. Other grants underwrite the employment of Community Health Representatives, tribe members hired to provide nursing, counseling, or ambulance service within the Otoe-Missouria community. Because these programs both serve the tribe and also employ many tribe members, they are particularly useful to the Otoe-Missouria people.

Visitors to the former Otoe-Missouria boarding school which now serves as the tribal center often find the buildings bustling with activity. The school contains the tribal offices and meeting rooms while the old laundry serves as a garage and storage area. Plans have been made for the renovation of other facilities and for the construction of a new, large multi-purpose center to be built on lands adjoining the old school grounds. In 1975, the tribe completed arrangements for the development of a new water system which will provide an ample water supply for the future.

Otoe-Missouria plans for the years ahead also include provisions for their children. Assisted by the United States Office of Education, during 1975-76

Photograph by Jerilyn Edmunds

IBAL CENTER. Once part of the Otoe-Missouria boarding school, these buildings near Red ck now house tribal offices and council chambers.

the tribe established a Pre-School Program open to all children in the Red Rock region. Meeting in the tribal center, Otoe-Missouria youngsters not only learn basic educational skills, they also are introduced to *Chiwere,* the traditional language of the Otoe-Missouria people. In 1975, the tribe produced *Let's Speak Chiwere,* an elementary grammar designed to familiarize tribal children with their native tongue. Additional volumes are planned for the near future and Tribal Executive Director Bill Burns is anxious to expand the tribe's entire educational program to include Otoe-Missouria youngsters of all ages.

In addition to the Otoe-Missouria language program, the tribe has made a conscious effort to continue another important tradition: the close association of the Otoe-Missouria people with "Che," the buffalo. During September, 1975, tribal officials acquired twenty animals from the government herd at Roosevelt National Park in North Dakota, and upon their arrival at Red Rock, the buffalo were pastured on Otoe-Missouria grazing lands near the tribal center. In the months that followed several bulls were slaughtered and the meat served at holidays or tribal celebrations, but in the spring of 1976 a calf was born, promising a bright future for the herd. With obvious pride in their ownership of the animals, many Otoe-Missourias look forward to increasing the herd when additional grazing lands have been purchased.

The continued interest of the Otoe-Missourias in

maintaining their traditional language and their close association with the buffalo testifies to the rich cultural heritage of the tribe. Although they are a people of the twentieth century, the Otoe-Missourias look back upon their past with a quiet pride reflected in the dignity of their elders' faces. Anxious to preserve their history, the tribe has decorated the center near Red Rock with paintings and photographs of prominent Otoe-Missourias from years gone by. Tribal leaders recently have collected records illustrating the Otoe-Missouria past, and during the spring of 1976 Truman Dailey and Bill De Hass traveled across Kansas and Nebraska gathering materials for an Otoe-Missouria history to be used in the tribe's educational programs. A film documenting the Otoe-Missouria's story also is under production.

Many of the old ways remain. Tribal elders still are revered and the Otoe-Missourias continue to be a generous people, willing to share their limited resources with friends or relatives who are in need. Some of the clans are gone but others endure and family relationships persist as one of the most cohesive forces within Otoe-Missouria society. Still a sociable people, tribal members meet regularly for hand games and other activities and once each year during July, most Otoe-Missourias assemble on the tribal campgrounds near Red Rock where they renew old acquaintances and participate in traditional dances and ceremonies.

Tempered by adversity, modern Otoe-Missourias have combined the best of their tribal values with

Photograph by Jerilyn Edmunds

FFALO HERD. Part of the Otoe-Missouria buffalo herd on tribal grazing lands near Red
ck. The Otoe-Missouria people traditionally relied upon the buffalo for food and other
cessities, and are building a tribal herd of these symbolically important animals.

many qualities from white society. Although their past has been darkened by hardship, most look forward to a brighter future. They are truly a people of two cultures.

SUGGESTED READING

With a few exceptions, scholars have written relatively little upon the history and culture of the Otoe-Missouria people. Although much information is available in government documents and in the manuscript collections of state and local historical societies, time and distance keep the majority of these records inaccessible to the general public. Most of the articles and books listed below should be available in large university or public libraries.

CHAPMAN, BERLIN B. "The Barnes Family of Barneston," *Nebraska History, XLVII* (March, 1966), 57-83.

An extended discussion of the Barnes family's role in Otoe-Missouria history, the article generally presents the Barnes family in favorable terms.

CHAPMAN, BERLIN B. *The Otoes and Missourias: A Study of Indian Removal and the Legal Aftermath.* Oklahoma City: Times Journal Publishing Company, 1965.

Written by the Otoe-Missouria's expert witness before the Indian Claims Commission, the volume is the most comprehensive study of the tribe after 1830. It contains detailed discussions of land cessions and subsequent litigation.

CHAPMAN, BERLIN B. "The Otoe and Missouria Reservation," *Chronicles of Oklahoma, XXVI* (Summer, 1948), 132-158.

This article describes the removal of the Otoe-Missouria people into Oklahoma and the subsequent allotment of reservation lands at Red Rock.

FOREMAN, GRANT. *The Last Trek of the Indians.* Chicago: University of Chicago Press, 1946.

Includes a short section upon the Otoe-Missouria removal and describes their plight within the general framework of nineteenth century Indian affairs.

HYDE, GEORGE. *Indians of the Woodlands From Prehistoric Times to 1725.* Norman: University of Oklahoma Press, 1962.

Offers an interesting, but speculative discussion of Otoe-Missouria prehistory.

MERRILL, MOSES. "Extracts From the Diary of Rev. Moses Merrill, A Missionary to the Otoe Indians From 1832 to 1840," *Transactions and Reports of the Nebraska State Historical Society.* Lincoln: State Journal Company, 1892. Vol. IV, 160-194.

Although this article contains only selected excerpts from Merrill's diary, it offers interesting descriptions of Otoe-Missouria culture during the 1830's. It also contains valuable insights into missionary attitudes during this period.

NASATIR, ABRAHAM P., ed. *Before Lewis and Clark.* 2 Vols. St. Louis: St. Louis Historical Documents Foundation, 1952.

Contain many documents providing invaluable information upon both the Otoe and Missouria tribes during the eighteenth century.

OTOE AND MISSOURIA INDIANS. New York: Garland Publishing Inc., 1974.

The volume contains material presented before the Indian Claims Commission. Much of the information is available in Chapman's *The Otoes and Missourias* listed above, but this volume includes a short section by an anonymous author discussing Otoe and Missouria tribal locations prior to 1820. The anonymous section disagrees with the traditional Otoe-Missouria migration legend.

THWAITES, REUBEN G., ed. *Early Western Travels.* 32 Vols. Cleveland: Arthur Clark Company, 1904-1907.

Scattered through this multi-volume work is much information on the Otoe-Missouria people. Edwin James' account of the Long Expedition, contained in volumes XIV-XVII is particularly valuable.

TREAT, JOHN IRVING. *Indian Sketches.* Edited by John Francis McDermott. Norman: University of Oklahoma Press, 1955.

Treat's journals include vivid descriptions of the Otoe-Missourias during the 1830's. His writings contain the best account of the Otoe chief, Iotan.

WHITMAN, WILLIAM. *The Oto.* New York: Columbia University Press, 1937.

This slim volume is the one best anthropological study of Otoe culture.

THE AUTHOR

A native of central Illinois, R. David Edmunds is an assistant professor of history at Texas Christian University. He holds a Ph.D. from the University of Oklahoma and also has taught at the University of Wyoming. The recipient of a Ford Foundation Fellowship and a Post-Doctoral Fellowship from the Center for the History of the American Indian, Professor Edmunds is the author of numerous articles in professional journals. He recently has completed a manuscript entitled "The Potawatomis: Keepers of the Fire," and is now writing a biography of the Shawnee Prophet. Among his future projects is a biography of the Otoe-Missouria chief, Iotan.